PEARSON EDEXCEL INTERNATIONAL GCSE (9–1)

HISTORY
THE USA, 1918–41
Student Book

Simon Davis

Series Editor: Nigel Kelly

Published by Pearson Education Limited, 80 Strand, London, WC2R 0RL.

www.pearsonglobalschools.com

Copies of official specifications for all Pearson qualifications may be found on the website: https://qualifications.pearson.com

Text © Pearson Education Limited 2017
Edited by Claire Smith, Jane Grisdale and Sarah Wright
Designed by Cobalt id and Pearson Education Limited
Typeset and illustrated by Phoenix Photosetting Ltd, Chatham, Kent
Original illustrations © Pearson Education Limited 2017
Cover design by Pearson Education Limited 2017
Picture research by Sarah Hewitt
Cover photo/illustration: **Mary Evans Picture Library/**Everett Collection
Inside front cover: **Shutterstock.com/**Dmitry Lobanov

The rights of Simon Davis to be identified as author of this work have been asserted by him in accordance with the Copyright, Designs and Patents Act 1988.

First published 2017

24

10 9 8

British Library Cataloguing in Publication Data
A catalogue record for this book is available from the British Library

ISBN 978 0 435 18545 9

Printed in Great Britain by Bell and Bain Ltd, Glasgow

Acknowledgements
The author and publisher would like to thank the following individuals and organisations for permission to reproduce photographs:
(Key: b-bottom; c-centre; l-left; r-right; t-top)

Alamy Stock Photo: akg-images 6, Everett Collection Historical 18, 52, Granger Historical Picture Archive 103, Photo Researchers, Inc 54, Pictorial Press Ltd 61, Sergey Skryl 73, The Granger Collection 31, World History Archive 13; **Bridgeman Art Library Ltd:** Private Collection / Peter Newark American Pictures 44; **Getty Images:** Bettmann 35, 49, 63, 74, 77b, 91, 98, Buyenlarge 27, David Pollack / Corbis 28, Edward G. Malindine / Topical Press Agency 2, Image Holdings / Corbis 86, Keystone-France / Gamma-Keystone 71, Library of Congress 76, 77tl, National Photo Company / Buyenlarge 21, Underwood Archives 84, Universal History Archive / UIG 81; **TopFoto:** Granger, NYC 41, 93, 95.

All other images © Pearson Education

We are grateful to the following for permission to reproduce copyright material:

Text
Extract on page 16 from *USA Between the Wars, 1919–41 (Discovering the Past for GCSE)*, Stu Rep ed., (White,C. and Samuelson,M. 1998) p.49, reproduced by permission of Hodder Education; Extracts on pages 34, 101, 109 from *Edexcel GCSE History A: The Making of the Modern World Unit 2C: The USA 1919–41*, (Shuter,J. 2013), Pearson Education Limited; Extract on page 45 from *Hodder Twentieth Century History: The USA, 1914–41*, (Mantin,P. 1997) p.18, reproduced by permission of Hodder Education; Extract on page 87 from *Franklin D. Roosevelt: The New Deal and War (Lancaster Pamphlets)*, Routledge (Heale,M.J. 1999) p.24; Extract on page 69 from *USA 1918–1941: Foundation Edition: Evaluation Pack (Heinemann Secondary History Project)*, (Kelly,N. 1997) p.41, Pearson Education Limited.

Select glossary terms have been taken from *The Longman Dictionary of Contemporary English Online*.

Disclaimer
All maps in this book are drawn to support the key learning points. They are illustrative in style and are not exact representations.

Endorsement Statement
In order to ensure that this resource offers high-quality support for the associated Pearson qualification, it has been through a review process by the awarding body. This process confirms that this resource fully covers the teaching and learning content of the specification or part of a specification at which it is aimed. It also confirms that it demonstrates an appropriate balance between the development of subject skills, knowledge and understanding, in addition to preparation for assessment.

Endorsement does not cover any guidance on assessment activities or processes (e.g. practice questions or advice on how to answer assessment questions), included in the resource nor does it prescribe any particular approach to the teaching or delivery of a related course.

While the publishers have made every attempt to ensure that advice on the qualification and its assessment is accurate, the official specification and associated assessment guidance materials are the only authoritative source of information and should always be referred to for definitive guidance.

Pearson examiners have not contributed to any sections in this resource relevant to examination papers for which they have responsibility.

Examiners will not use endorsed resources as a source of material for any assessment set by Pearson. Endorsement of a resource does not mean that the resource is required to achieve this Pearson qualification, nor does it mean that it is the only suitable material available to support the qualification, and any resource lists produced by the awarding body shall include this and other appropriate resources.

ABOUT THIS BOOK

This book is written for students following the Pearson Edexcel International GCSE (9–1) History specification and covers one unit of the course. This unit is The USA, 1918–41, one of the Historical Investigations.

The History course has been structured so that teaching and learning can take place in any order, both in the classroom and in any independent learning. The book contains five chapters which match the five areas of content in the specification:
- The Roaring Twenties
- Increased social tensions in the 1920s
- The USA in Depression, 1929–33
- Roosevelt and the New Deal, 1933–41
- The Opposition to the New Deal

Each chapter is split into multiple sections to break down content into manageable chunks and to ensure full coverage of the specification.

Each chapter features a mix of learning and activities. Sources are embedded throughout to develop your understanding and exam-style questions help you to put learning into practice. Recap pages at the end of each chapter summarise key information and let you check your understanding. Exam guidance pages help you prepare confidently for the exam.

Learning objectives
Each section starts with a list of what you will learn in it. They are carefully tailored to address key assessment objectives central to the course.

Extend your knowledge
Interesting facts to encourage wider thought and stimulate discussion. They are closely related to key issues and allow you to add depth to your knowledge and answers.

Timeline
Visual representation of events to clarify the order in which they happened.

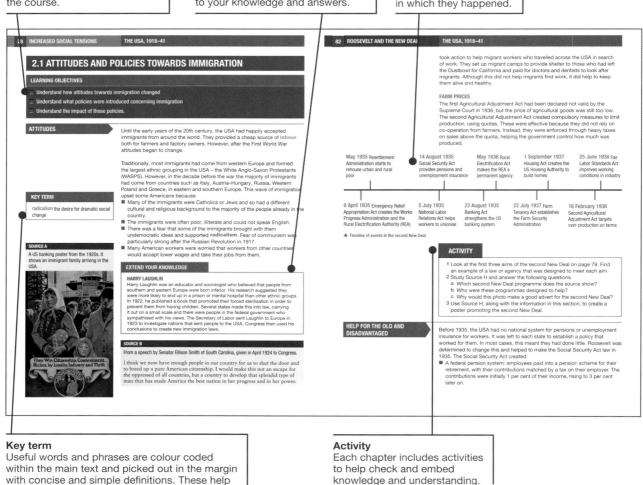

Key term
Useful words and phrases are colour coded within the main text and picked out in the margin with concise and simple definitions. These help understanding of key subject terms and support students whose first language is not English.

Activity
Each chapter includes activities to help check and embed knowledge and understanding.

Exam-style question
Questions tailored to the Pearson Edexcel specification to allow for practice and development of exam writing technique. They also allow for practice responding to the command words used in the exams.

Skills
Relevant exam questions have been assigned the key skills which you will gain from undertaking them, allowing for a strong focus on particular academic qualities. These transferable skills are highly valued in further study and the workplace.

Source
Photos, cartoons and text sources are used to explain events and show you what people from the period said, thought or created, helping you to build your understanding.

Hint
All exam-style questions are accompanied by a hint to help you get started on an answer.

Recap
At the end of each chapter, you will find a page designed to help you consolidate and reflect on the chapter as a whole.

Recall quiz
This quick quiz is ideal for checking your knowledge or for revision.

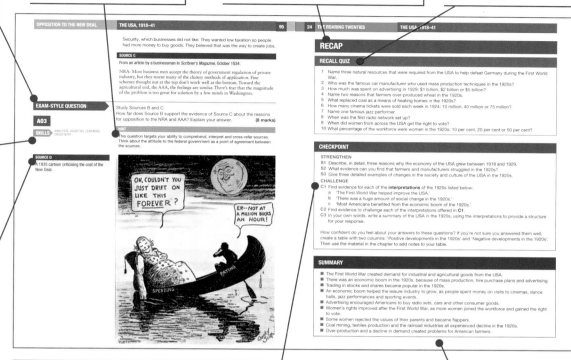

Checkpoint
Checkpoints help you to check and reflect on your learning. The Strengthen section helps you to consolidate knowledge and understanding, and check that you have grasped the basic ideas and skills. The Challenge questions push you to go beyond just understanding the information, and into evaluation and analysis of what you have studied.

Summary
The main points of each chapter are summarised in a series of bullet points. These are great for embedding core knowledge and handy for revision.

Exam guidance
At the end of each chapter, you will find two pages designed to help you better understand the exam questions and how to answer them. Each exam guidance section focuses on a particular question type that you will find in the exam, allowing you to approach them with confidence.

Student answers
Exemplar student answers are used to show what an answer to the exam question may look like. There are often two levels of answers so you can see what you need to do to write better responses.

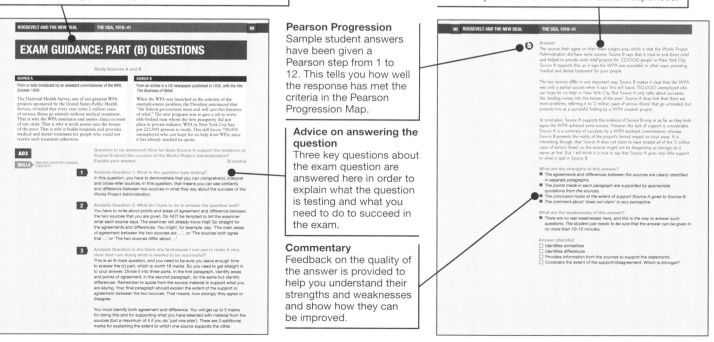

Pearson Progression
Sample student answers have been given a Pearson step from 1 to 12. This tells you how well the response has met the criteria in the Pearson Progression Map.

Advice on answering the question
Three key questions about the exam question are answered here in order to explain what the question is testing and what you need to do to succeed in the exam.

Commentary
Feedback on the quality of the answer is provided to help you understand their strengths and weaknesses and show how they can be improved.

TIMELINE – THE USA, 1918–41

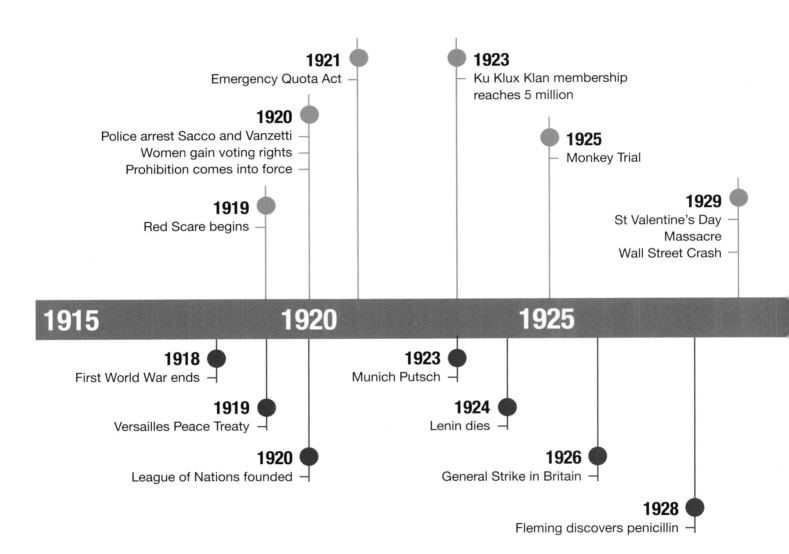

1921
Emergency Quota Act

1923
Ku Klux Klan membership reaches 5 million

1920
Police arrest Sacco and Vanzetti
Women gain voting rights
Prohibition comes into force

1925
Monkey Trial

1919
Red Scare begins

1929
St Valentine's Day Massacre
Wall Street Crash

1915   **1920**   **1925**

1918
First World War ends

1923
Munich Putsch

1919
Versailles Peace Treaty

1924
Lenin dies

1920
League of Nations founded

1926
General Strike in Britain

1928
Fleming discovers penicillin

TIMELINE – WORLD

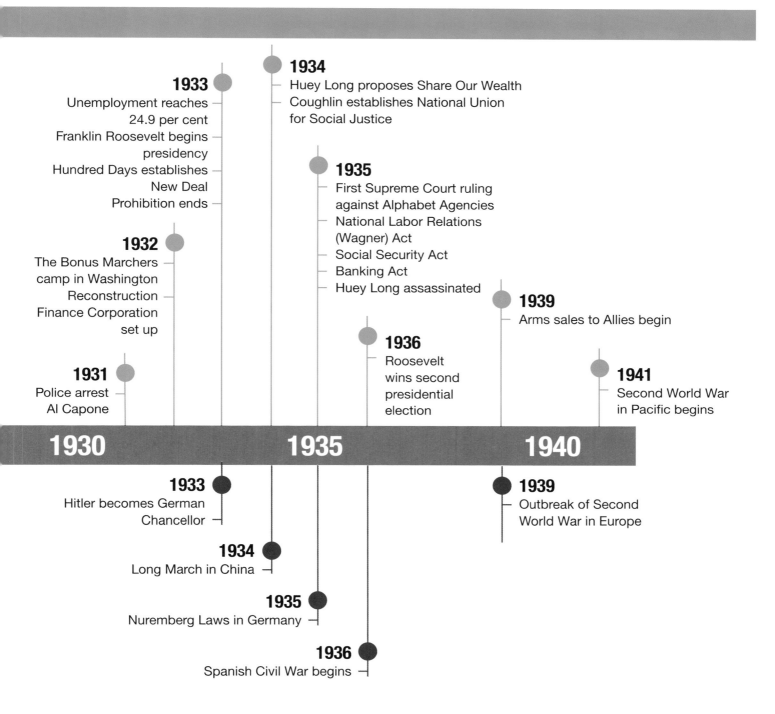

1934
Huey Long proposes Share Our Wealth
Coughlin establishes National Union
for Social Justice

1933
Unemployment reaches
24.9 per cent
Franklin Roosevelt begins
presidency
Hundred Days establishes
New Deal
Prohibition ends

1935
First Supreme Court ruling
against Alphabet Agencies
National Labor Relations
(Wagner) Act
Social Security Act
Banking Act
Huey Long assassinated

1932
The Bonus Marchers
camp in Washington
Reconstruction
Finance Corporation
set up

1939
Arms sales to Allies begin

1931
Police arrest
Al Capone

1936
Roosevelt
wins second
presidential
election

1941
Second World War
in Pacific begins

1930   **1935**   **1940**

1933
Hitler becomes German
Chancellor

1939
Outbreak of Second
World War in Europe

1934
Long March in China

1935
Nuremberg Laws in Germany

1936
Spanish Civil War begins

1. THE ROARING TWENTIES

LEARNING OBJECTIVES

- ☐ Understand the reasons why America experienced an economic boom after the First World War
- ☐ Understand the changes in society and culture that the USA experienced in the 1920s, including the changing position of women
- ☐ Understand the problems in farming and the decline of older industries.

The 1920s was a decade of contrasts. On the one hand, the economy grew quickly. The First World War had created demand for US goods, factories had new methods of production and ordinary people could use cheap loans to buy the goods they heard about in radio commercials. With a radio set in most homes and a cinema in most towns, the USA had national forms of entertainment for the first time. They also had more leisure time, which meant more people went to watch sporting events or attended dances and jazz clubs.

On the other hand, there was a darker side to what was known as the 'Roaring Twenties'. Some farmers went bankrupt, as they produced more food than was needed for a world no longer at war. Factory workers in the 'older industries', such as textile mills and engineering, also struggled, as the products they made were replaced with newer ones. These workers had to accept lower wages and the threat of losing their jobs. Although women had greater freedoms in the 1920s, they still suffered inequalities in pay and employment opportunities – and for many, life continued to be a struggle running the family home and looking after children.

1.1 THE USA IN 1918

LEARNING OBJECTIVES

- Understand the geography of the USA at the end of the First World War
- Understand the key features of US society in 1918
- Understand the way in which the USA was governed.

WHAT DID THE USA LOOK LIKE?

The United States of America was a big country of over 9 million square km. It stretched across an entire continent, was bordered by Canada to its north and Mexico to its south and was divided into 48 states. Within its land borders, it was a nation of farms, but its cities had begun to grow in size. Beyond them, there was a small US empire, with island colonies in places like Hawaii and Puerto Rico.

WHO LIVED THERE?

Its people, numbering around 105 million, were from a range of ethnic backgrounds. New immigrants were still arriving from Europe, Latin America and Asia in the early 20th century, in search of work or to escape persecution. They joined a population that included the descendants of European settlers who had founded the USA, as well as the African Americans the settlers had used as slaves and the Native Americans, whose land the settlers had taken.

This diversity made the USA something of a melting pot for different cultures, sometimes creating tension between them. Many groups faced persecution, including:
- African Americans: many had only received freedom from slavery after the American Civil War (1861–65) and the USA was still a deeply racist society.

▼ **Figure 1.1** A map of the USA in 1918

- Native Americans: most had ended up living in reservations, as their ancestral lands were taken from them by US settlers.
- New immigrants: the USA introduced laws to reduce immigration in the late 19th and early 20th centuries. For example, entry from Japan was **restricted** in 1900.

HOW IS THE USA RUN?

Powers

Federal
- Declare war
- Armed forces
- Foreign policy
- Regulate interstate trade
- The currency

Shared
- Law and order
- Taxes
- Court system
- Regulate banks
- Public welfare

State
- Education
- Local government
- Regulate trade within the state
- Marriage laws

Structure

Legislative (Congress)
- Passes laws
- Agrees taxes
- Agrees president's appointments of judges and ministers

Executive (President)
- Proposes laws
- Runs foreign policy
- Appoints government ministers
- Commands armed forces

Judicial (Supreme Court)
- Interprets constitution and laws
- Final appeal court

Checks and balances

President
- Checks Congress because can veto laws
- Checks Supreme Court because president appoints judges

Congress
- Checks president's power because can reject appointments or overturn the president's veto, and can withhold taxes
- Checks Supreme Court because can pass new laws and change the constitution (if states agree)

Supreme Court
- Checks president because can say actions are unconstitutional
- Checks Congress because can say actions are unconstitutional

▶ **Figure 1.2** The US system of government

The USA has a federal system of government. Power is divided between the federal (central) government in Washington DC and the state governments, which meet in each of the states in the USA (see Figure 1.2). It is a republic that is divided into three parts:

- an elected president who sets policy
- an elected Congress that makes laws
- an appointed Supreme Court that checks laws are in keeping with the constitution.

This three-part system was designed to make sure that no one person or group had too much power, because each part can check the actions of the other (see Figure 1.2). Even so, shortly after the US government was designed, political parties that shared the same views and priorities began to emerge. By 1918, there were two main parties:

- the Republican Party that wanted government to play a small role in the lives of its citizens, allowing businesses to grow and succeed
- the Democratic Party that wanted government to play a larger role in the lives of its citizens, in order to tackle the social problems they faced.

This two-party system made voting simpler, but it also meant that if one party controlled all three parts of the government, they could gain more power.

1.2 THE ECONOMIC BENEFITS OF THE FIRST WORLD WAR

LEARNING OBJECTIVES

- Understand the impact of the First World War on US industry
- Understand the effect of European demand for food during the First World War on US agriculture
- Understand the problems created by the end of the First World War for the US economy and society.

KEY TERMS

submarines underwater vehicles used by the German navy during the First World War to attack enemy supply passenger and military ships, including, from February 1917, US ships

telegram a short message sent using electrical signals along a wire

When the First World War began in 1914, the US government said it would not take sides, but American support for Britain and France soon became clear. America offered huge loans to help Britain and France keep fighting and sold them far more goods than they shipped to Germany. However, it was not until 1917 that US President Woodrow Wilson felt he had to declare war. German submarines had begun to attack US ships and a secret telegram was discovered, revealing a German plot against the USA. As a result, on 2 April 1917, the president declared war on Germany and its allies.

By this point the war had already had a massive effect on the US economy, because it had created demand for American goods in Europe. Europeans involved in the war did not have time to grow enough food, extract enough fuel, or produce enough iron and steel. The Americans, who were a long way from the fighting itself, provided these resources. As a result, their industries, farms and workers benefited from a huge growth in overseas demand.

INDUSTRY

During the First World War, factory production in America grew by 35 per cent. One of the largest areas of growth was in the steel industry. In 1910, America had produced 26.1 million tonnes of steel. This had increased to 42.1 million tonnes by 1920. Other industries also experienced expansion, including those involved in:

■ Natural resources: the industries involved in coal, petrol and gas production all grew quickly.
■ Transport: shipbuilding increased to replace ships destroyed by submarines and the railroads were modernised to transport wartime goods and soldiers around the USA efficiently.
■ Consumer goods: American brands, especially the cigarettes smoked by US soldiers, became very popular in Europe.

SOURCE A

A poster from 1917 produced by the US Shipping Board. It shows a worker in a shipyard.

AGRICULTURE

Production on US farms grew rapidly during the First World War. Many European farmers had to fight in the war and production in Europe dropped. This created huge global demand for agricultural goods, including wheat for food production and cotton for clothing. This meant that by the time Europe had begun to recover from the war, America supplied 30 per cent of the world's wheat and 55 per cent of its cotton, which changed the lives of farmers in a number of ways:

- prices for their goods rose by around 25 per cent during the war
- the average income of a farmer who owned their farm increased by around 30 per cent
- farmers began to use machines on their farms and tractor sales increased dramatically
- more and more farmers took out loans in order to expand their farms to increase production of wheat to sell abroad.

WORKERS

The war had a number of positive impacts on American workers. Firstly, demand for more industrial and agricultural goods meant more workers were needed. As a result, the number of people in work increased by 1.3 million during the last 2 years of the war, reducing unemployment. Secondly, most workers benefited from wage increases. For example, the wages of unskilled workers rose by around 20 per cent during the war. Finally, there were more opportunities for workers from a range of backgrounds, because they were needed to replace the men who had gone to fight in Europe. Many women joined the **workforce** and black Americans moved from agriculture in the southern states into industrial jobs in the northern ones.

LIMITATIONS

EXTEND YOUR KNOWLEDGE

RACE RIOTS
During the war, black people from the southern states continued to face poverty and racism, so the idea of an escape appealed to them. An opportunity arose when businesses, whose workers had gone to fight in the war, encouraged them to move north. Around 400,000 did so. However, they did not escape racism. White workers, who did not like the new workers, looked for any excuse to attack black communities. For example, in 1917, 40 black people and nine white people were killed in a race riot in Illinois.

The First World War had transformed the American economy, its workers and its global trade for the better. However, there were problems at the end of the war:

- Government contracts were cancelled and European farming had recovered by 1920. Demand for industrial and agricultural products from the USA dropped as a result.
- Returning soldiers re-entered the workforce. Many new workers, mainly women, lost their wartime jobs as a consequence.
- The increased number of black workers in some industrial cities had caused race **riots**, which continued after the war.
- Farmers who had borrowed money to expand production struggled to pay back their loans, especially as European demand began to drop (see pages 20–21).

ACTIVITY

1 Look at Source A. Discuss with a partner one way it could be improved.
2 Read back through the text on pages 5–7 and identify another area of the economy that required more workers. Write a short design brief for a poster to attract workers to your chosen area.
3 Swap your brief with a partner. They should create a poster that meets your requirements.
4 Pass the posters around the class. Each time you see a way the US economy changed during the war, make a note of it.

1.3 REASONS FOR ECONOMIC BOOM IN THE 1920S

LEARNING OBJECTIVES

- Understand the importance of mass production and hire purchase for the US economy
- Understand the contribution of advertising and consumerism to the economic boom in the 1920s
- Understand the significance of the popularity of the stock market on the economy.

KEY TERMS

boom period when the economy is growing and unemployment is low

credit money loaned by a bank to a customer for a fixed period of time, usually repaid in instalments along with an additional amount called interest

shares evidence of ownership of part of a company, allowing the holder to receive a portion of any profit made by the company, known as a dividend

After 1922, America was experiencing an economic **boom**. This came about as a result of:

- new production methods that allowed factories to produce goods at a faster rate
- the availability of **credit** to buy new things
- advertising that encouraged people to buy newly available consumer goods
- the increased popularity of investing in stocks and **shares**.

The average income of an American was rising, while the number of hours they were expected to work was falling. Unemployment was also low, never rising above 3.7 per cent until 1929.

HENRY FORD AND MASS PRODUCTION

EXTEND YOUR KNOWLEDGE

MASS PRODUCTION
Most people think Ford invented mass production, because his publicity secretary wrote the first entry on it in the *Encyclopaedia Britannica* in 1926. However, it has a longer history. Ideas about the use of machinery in production came from the 18th-century textiles industry, along with ideas about standardised parts from the weapons industry and the organisation of mass production methods from the steel industry. Ford put these ideas together and added a conveyor belt.

Before Henry Ford introduced mass production techniques, it took 12 hours for skilled workers to produce a Model T car in a **workshop**. Mass production changed this. The idea was that workers lined up along a continuously moving surface called a conveyor belt. The car would travel along the belt as each worker stayed in the same place and performed a single job, like fitting a part or a bolt to the body of the car. This was extremely boring for the worker, but it meant that production time fell. On one of Ford's most efficient days, 31 October 1925, a Model T car was produced every 10 seconds.

The result of these **innovations** was a tremendous drop in price. More cars were made per day, so they could be sold more cheaply. The original cost of the Model T car was $950, but by 1925 it cost only $290. The result was a huge increase in the demand for cars amongst Americans. This helped the economy to boom because the construction of cars required the products of other industries, including steel, rubber, glass and textiles, while the use of cars boosted demand for petrol and roads. The lives of Americans themselves were affected by the increase in car ownership, which is explored on page 15.

HIRE PURCHASE

In 1919, Alfred Sloan set up a credit agency designed for ordinary consumers. His company, and others like it, helped people to get products they wanted without having to save up for them. The idea was that the customer hired the product from the business, paying for it in **instalments**. Once they had paid off the cost in full, the product became theirs. It became known as 'hire purchase'.

Hire purchase, along with the confidence to pay off the instalments that came from secure employment, helped the economy because it encouraged people to keep buying. In 1929, 75 per cent of cars and 50 per cent of electrical devices were bought using hire purchase. With more consumers buying goods, demand rose and factories had a reason to keep producing.

ADVERTISING

In the 1920s, advertising became a big business. Companies, like Kellogg's Corn Flakes, used big posters and colour pages in newspapers and magazines to encourage people to buy their products. They tried to overwhelm consumers with images of their brands in order to change their buying habits. Some companies went even further, trying to create new markets for their goods. For example, Listerine popularised the term 'halitosis' for bad breath, then rebranded their product, previously sold as an antiseptic, as a mouthwash to cure the condition. Later on, they even tried to market Listerine as a deodorant.

SOURCE B

From an article about advertising published in 1925.

Advertising does give a certain illusion, a certain sense of escape in a machine age. It creates a dream world: smiling faces, shining teeth, schoolgirl complexions, cornless feet, perfect fitting suits, distinguished collars, wrinkleless trousers, odourless breaths, regularized bowels, happy homes, fast motors, punctureless tires, perfect busts and self-washing dishes.

Radio also played a central role in the development of advertising. By 1929, there were 618 radio stations and most of these carried adverts, or were sponsored by big brand names. For example, a New York City radio programme, which started in 1923, was called the *Eveready Hour*, because it was sponsored by the battery maker. It was a light entertainment programme, based around a weekly theme, but also advertised their products. As a result, Americans even spent their leisure time listening to adverts.

By 1929, $2 billion a year was spent on advertising and 600,000 people were employed in the industry. New advertising methods helped to create a consumer society in the 1920s, encouraging people to buy new products, or spend more on brand names. This again boosted the economy because more spending created a need for increased production. More production meant more jobs, which meant more people had money to spend.

CONSUMERISM

SOURCE C

From an article about advertising by Earnest Elmo Calkins published in 1928.

Sometimes advertising supplies a demand, but in most cases it creates demand for things that were beyond even the imagination of those who would benefit from them the most. A woman knew the use of a broom, but she could not imagine a vacuum cleaner. Therefore she could not demand one, save with that vague unspoken desire for some easing of the terrible hard work of keeping a house clean and tidy.

Advertisers and **marketing** companies actively tried to encourage **consumerism** and create a consumer society in which buying a variety of branded goods was important to ordinary people. While previously people had always washed their handkerchiefs, now Kimberley Clark sold consumers one that you could throw away. Rather than eat one flavour of yoghurt or colour their hair in a couple of shades, people were encouraged to buy an assortment of yoghurts from a range of flavours and choose from ten different hair colours.

Shopping quickly became a leisure activity. As America grew richer, people wanted to show they were better off than their neighbours and they could do this by buying the new consumer goods. By 1929 there were 1,395 department stores to choose from and sales of all sorts of goods rose rapidly. For example, 5,000 refrigerators were sold in 1921. By 1929, this had risen to 1 million. Consumers also spent huge amounts on home entertainment, with $850 million per year being spent on radio equipment. People were now buying things they had not even realised they needed a decade before, which helped the economy to keep growing.

EXAM-STYLE QUESTION

A03

SKILLS ANALYSIS, ADAPTIVE LEARNING, CREATIVITY

Study Sources B and C.
How far does Source B support the evidence of Source C about the effect of advertising in the USA in the 1920s? Explain your answer. **(8 marks)**

HINT

This question targets your ability to comprehend, interpret and cross-refer sources. Consider what Source B means by 'illusion' when you are looking for a point of disagreement.

STOCK MARKET POPULARITY

Between 1927 and 1929, 1.5 million ordinary Americans became involved in buying shares in the American stock market in Wall Street, New York. They either used their own money, or a method called 'buying on the margin', to buy shares in a company. This involved borrowing money from a bank, or **broker**, to invest in shares. Once they sold the shares, usually at a profit, they could pay back the loan (see Figure 1.3).

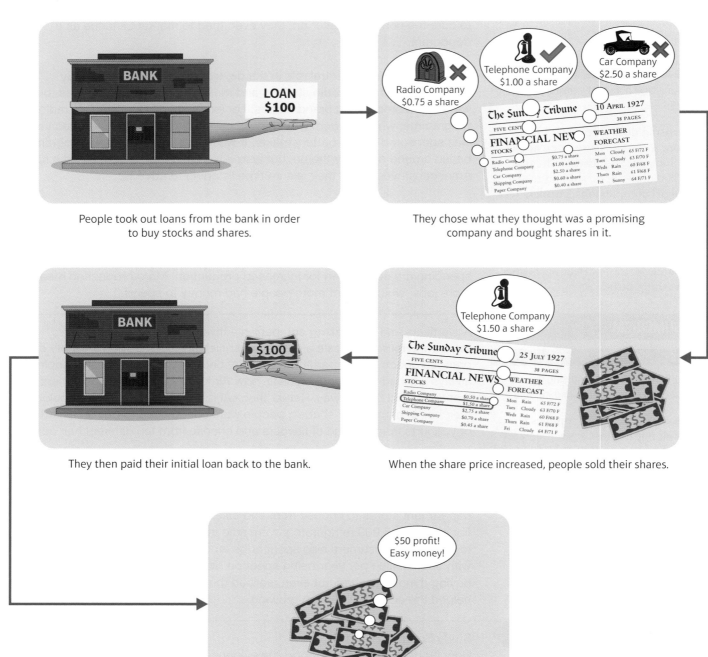

People took out loans from the bank in order to buy stocks and shares.

They chose what they thought was a promising company and bought shares in it.

They then paid their initial loan back to the bank.

When the share price increased, people sold their shares.

The rest of the money from selling the shares was the person's profit.

▲ **Figure 1.3** 'Buying on the margin'

These practices turned ordinary people into **shareholders**. Each shareholder did this in the hope that the value of the share would go up and they could sell it at a profit. They were confident share prices would rise because they had been going up since 1927. But it was a dangerous game, because ordinary Americans were effectively gambling on shares rising to make money quickly and repay their loans. What would happen if share prices stopped going up? Or even fell?

At first this helped the economy to grow. There was a huge amount of buying and selling in the stock market, which meant share prices kept on rising, as shown in the following table.

COMPANY	3 MARCH 1928	3 SEPTEMBER 1929
Woolworths	$1.81	$2.51
Radio Corp.	$0.94	$5.05
AT & T (telephone company)	$0.77	$3.04
Westinghouse (electrical company)	$0.92	$2.89
General Motors (cars)	$1.40	$1.82

It also led more companies to sell shares, which would give them the money they needed to develop their business. In 1925, there were around 500,000 shares available to buy on the stock market, but by 1929 there were 1,127,000. As a result, there were more businesses that had more money available to them. They were able to hire more people, providing them with money to invest in shares, or buy consumer goods with, resulting in greater profit. Ordinary people continued to invest and the economy continued to boom.

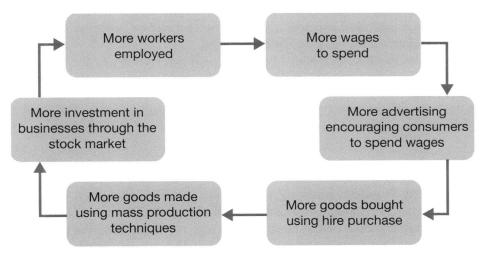

▲ **Figure 1.4** The boom cycle

ACTIVITY

1 In groups of four, assign each person one of the causes of the economic boom on pages 8–11.
2 On A4 paper, create a three-box flow diagram for your cause. In the first box write in the cause, with some historical detail, and in the third put 'An economic boom in the USA'. In the second box, try and briefly explain how the cause led to the boom.
3 Share your findings with the rest of your group. Then place the flow diagrams in a row in order of their importance in causing the economic boom. Discuss the reasons behind your decisions.

1.4 THE SOCIAL IMPACT OF THE ROARING TWENTIES

LEARNING OBJECTIVES

- Understand the impact of the economic boom on American society, including the leisure industry, cinema, jazz music, dancing and sport
- Understand the importance of radio, advertising and motoring for the way Americans used their leisure time
- Understand the importance of the 1920s for the position of women in society, including the impact of the flappers.

As a result of the economic boom, Americans had more money to spend and more leisure time. Their average income had risen by 30 per cent in the 1920s, but they worked fewer hours to earn it.

THE LEISURE INDUSTRY

For those Americans who could afford it, the 1920s was a decade where people spent more time on leisure activities than they had since the USA was founded in the 18th century. In fact, Americans spent $1.8 billion more on their leisure activities in 1929 than they had 10 years before. They bought new radio equipment, attended sports events and watched films at the cinema.

CINEMA

Movies grew very popular in the 1920s. In 1924, around 40 million cinema tickets were sold each week. This figure had more than doubled by 1929 because the film industry did everything they could to attract more viewers:

- They produced films in colour: by 1922, the Technicolor Corporation had come up with a way to produce colour films.
- They introduced sound: early films were silent and sometimes accompanied by live musicians. In 1927, the first film with sound, *The Jazz Singer*, was released.
- They developed animation techniques: Walt Disney's *Steamboat Willy* was the first movie to achieve general success with this technique in 1928.

The result of these developments was that, even though Americans did not have televisions in their homes, most saw films on a weekly basis at their local cinema. This generated huge profits for the film industry, which sold around $2 billion in cinema tickets each year, and provided another way by which advertising could reach consumers. It also made celebrities of men like Rudolph Valentino, who became an idol for millions of young Americans, and Charlie Chaplin, who entertained audiences with his comic acting.

EXTEND YOUR KNOWLEDGE

HAYS CODE

In response to criticism that the film industry was immoral, Hollywood studios appointed Will H. Hays to help clean up films. He developed a production code that, amongst other things, banned the filming of long kisses, childbirth and sex between white and black people. It said that religion had to be treated with respect so churchmen could not be villains and it restricted the presentation of certain crimes, like detailed descriptions of murdering someone, to avoid the audience copying things they had seen. The Hays Code remained in force until the rating system was introduced in 1968.

SOURCE D

A photo from 1927 of a crowd of people queuing up to see *The Jazz Singer*. Vitaphone was the system used to synchronise the sound and picture.

JAZZ AND DANCING

Writer F. Scott Fitzgerald called the 1920s the 'Jazz Age' because of the growing popularity of this form of music. Jazz was a mixture of black and white American folk music that had developed in multi-racial cities, like New Orleans, across the USA

Jazz soon became popular around the world. This was thanks to the international fame of men like Duke Ellington, who performed at the Cotton Club in New York City, and Paul Whiteman, who introduced symphonic jazz performed by a white orchestra. As a consequence, jazz became popular with white and black people and made big stars of people like Louis Armstrong and Kid Ory. However, it also created opposition, because it was associated with immoral behaviour amongst younger people.

Jazz music helped to inspire new forms of dancing. The Charleston was a fast dance, involving side kicks and a complex sequence of steps. It had originally been performed by a solo dancer, but became a popular group dance in the 1920s. This was a result of its promotion by on-screen stars, like Joan Crawford, who danced the Charleston in the 1928 film, *Our Dancing Daughter*.

Another popular dance was the Black Bottom. Like the Charleston, it was a fast and energetic style and it became popular thanks to a show called *George White's Scandals*, which ran from 1919 to 1939. It was just one of a number of dances that spread to ballrooms and dance halls across the USA and resulted in a new form of competition. This was called marathon dancing and was a test of fitness. Couples had to keep dancing until everyone else had stopped due to exhaustion. The last to remain on their feet were the winners.

EXTEND YOUR KNOWLEDGE

DEATH DANCE

The Charleston gained a reputation as a 'death dance', because it was such an energetic form of dancing it caused buildings to fall down. In July 1925, the dance floor of Boston's Pickwick Club collapsed, the walls caved in and 44 people died. The Charleston was blamed, but it is more likely that previous fire damage, along with poor repairs, led to the tragedy.

SPORT

More leisure time meant that Americans could spend their holidays, weekends and spare hours watching their favourite sports. This became a very popular hobby for thousands of people. For example, in 1921, 300,000 people went to watch the baseball World Series. The popularity of baseball, along with a range of other sports (see Figure 1.5), helped to create a huge number of sporting heroes in the 1920s.

Baseball: Babe Ruth set a record of 60 home runs, which remained unbeaten until 1961.

Boxing: Jack Dempsey fought Gene Turney in the Long Count Fight (1927) that took $2 million in ticket sales.

Golf: Bobby Jones was the first golfer to achieve a Grand Slam in the major golf tournaments of 1930.

Swimming: Gertrude Ederle, a US swimmer, became the first woman to swim the English Channel in 1926.

Tennis: Bill Tilden became a well known player, winning seven US championships.

American football: Red Grange helped popularise the sport and was known as the 'Galloping Ghost' due to his speed.

▲ **Figure 1.5** Sporting heroes of the 1920s

RADIO AND ADVERTISING

Radio in the 1920s became just as important in people's homes as television and the internet are today. The number of radios in the USA grew from 60,000 in 1920 to 10 million in 1929. These broadcast a range of shows, including comedies like *Amos 'n' Andy*, sport commentaries and live music. At first, there were hundreds of local stations, but these became part of networks from the late 1920s onwards. For example, the National Broadcasting Corporation (NBC) was set up in 1926. This helped to combine the material used by many stations so that people across the USA began to hear similar views, news and adverts for the first time.

The rise of this technology also meant that Americans spent part of their leisure time listening to adverts, which influenced how they used their spare time. Some women began to spend their free hours buying Max Factor make-up and applying it so that they could look like movie stars. People took up new hobbies, like photography, using their new Kodak cameras. And they changed their expectations of how people would smell when they turned up at the dance hall, because Colgate encouraged them to brush their teeth and Listerine suggested they wash their mouth as well.

MOTORING

Car ownership changed a lot in the 1920s. At the start of the decade, 8 million people owned motor cars, but by 1929 this number had risen to 23 million. Henry Ford's Model T car was largely responsible for this rise, but its low price meant the car only came in one design and one colour. His competitors saw a gap in the market and began to turn motoring into a hobby by offering a greater variety of models. For example, General Motors produced a more expensive car called the K Model Chevrolet in 1925. From then on, car ownership, maintenance and driving became a leisure activity, rather than simply a way of getting around.

Ford's cheap car brought new possibilities to ordinary Americans. They could now travel greater distances, in shorter times, at lower prices. This had a number of effects on how they spent their leisure time, because it meant:
- It was easier to go on holidays or day trips: the number of visitors to American national parks went up from 198,606 in 1910 to 2.7 million in 1930.
- Bargain hunters could visit suburban shopping centres: plans for the first such development, in Kansas City, began in 1922.
- Major cities were in reach of more people: residents of rural areas felt less remote, because they could take part in social activities held in nearby cities.

ACTIVITY

1 Write three bullet-pointed notes to summarise one of these topics: cinema, jazz, dancing, sport, radio, advertising or motoring.
2 Create a table on A4 paper with two columns, 'Features' and 'Notes', and an empty row for each of the topics listed above.
3 Find someone who has made notes on a different topic. Without showing your notes, explain to each other your topics. You should write a few notes while your partner is talking.
4 Find a new partner and repeat the process a few times. Then return to your original seat and work in pairs to fill in any remaining gaps in your table.

THE POSITION OF WOMEN IN 1918

JOBS

The First World War had helped to improve the position of women in the workforce, because they were needed to replace the men who went to fight. During the course of the war, women made up 20 per cent of the workforce in work places such as weapons factories and steel mills. However, most women still worked in jobs seen as traditionally female, mainly in low-paid service work, as shop assistants and secretaries. It was also expected that women, unless they were from a poor background, would not continue to work after they got married.

RIGHTS

Women's political rights had begun to improve by 1918. Some states had given women the right to vote in local and state elections, such as New York, which passed a law to allow this in November 1917. Despite this progress, many American women did not have the vote or the same employment opportunities, right to equal pay and legal rights as men.

LIFESTYLE

Most people thought that women should do the household jobs, follow their husband's instructions and behave respectably. This meant many women spent their days cooking, cleaning and raising children. If they went out, many people expected them to be accompanied by a **chaperone** and not to drink or smoke.

IMPROVEMENTS FOR WOMEN

JOBS

During the 1920s, women made progress in the world of work. Their situation improved in the following ways:
- There were more women workers: 2 million women joined the workforce, which meant they made up about 20 per cent of its total.
- They had access to different types of jobs: in one study, women were found in 537 of 572 different types of jobs available.
- More married women worked: their number increased from 1.9 million to 3.1 million during the 1920s.

RIGHTS

In 1920, the Nineteenth **Amendment** of the US Constitution gave women the right to vote. As a result, the government began to pass more laws that reflected the interests of women. For example, the Sheppard–Towner Act of 1921 provided health care services with the money needed to support pregnant women through local health centres. In addition to new laws designed to help women, some women even became politicians. In 1928, there were 145 women in state governments, which gave them a voice that they did not have before 1920.

LIFESTYLE

Women's freedom increased in the 1920s. The divorce rate rose, from 10 per cent to around 17 per cent, while the birth rate fell to 21.3 births per 1,000 people. There was also an increasing number of electrical appliances, such as the vacuum cleaner, which made household jobs easier. Fewer women felt they had to stay in failing relationships, look after several children and spend hours sweeping the house. They had more leisure time and some even rebelled against tradition and became **flappers** (see pages 18–19).

LIMITATIONS

Although women made considerable progress in their work and home life, as well as in politics, there were limits to this. Figure 1.6 illustrates some of the challenges that women still faced at the end of the 1920s.

KEY TERM

amendment an addition to, or alteration of, the US Constitution, of which there have been 27 since the introduction of the Constitution in 1789

EXTRACT A

From a history of the USA published in 1998.

Some of the social restrictions women had faced before the war had weakened. Before the war, women had been expected to have long hair. After the war, short hair became a sign of liberation. Make-up became popular and sales boomed, led by advertisements. In the 1920s, women smoked in public and drove cars, both of which would have been frowned upon before the war. Middle-class women had more free time, partly through the new domestic labour-saving products like vacuum cleaners. If they had a car (as many did) they were no longer so bound to the home.

Jobs

Most women were still in traditionally female jobs, working as secretaries or bookkeepers.

Only 12% of married women had jobs at the end of the 1920s.

Racial minority women remained in the lowest paid jobs, often as domestic servants.

Rights

Most women did not use their vote to gain more power by voting as a group, but instead followed their husband's decision.

Only two women were in the House of Representatives, part of the central government, in 1928.

Women did not achieve equal pay. In December 1927, the average woman earned around $12 less than a man each week.

Lifestyle

Women were still expected to look after the home and her children.

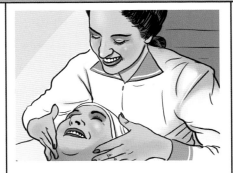

There were 40,000 beauty parlours by 1930, but this was a distraction from gaining more rights.

The proportion of women who attended higher education, compared to men, fell in the 1920s.

▲ **Figure 1.6** The limitations to women's progress in the 1920s

SOURCE E

From the account of a spinner, written in 1930, of the lives of textile mill workers in North Carolina.

The married women of the South get up at about five to take the cow out to the pasture, do some weeding in the garden, and they always have hot cakes for their husband's breakfast when he arises. Then they prepare their children for school and finally start work in the mill at 6:30 to work eleven hours. Upon their return to their homes they have housework to do.

THE FLAPPERS

EXTEND YOUR KNOWLEDGE

BEACH ARRESTS

Flappers often wore revealing swimwear when they visited a beach, which showed a lot of leg or chest. In response, some states passed dress code laws, meaning that flappers could be arrested for their fashion choices. One widely reported case involved a 39-year-old novelist called Louise Rosine, who refused to follow the rules on a beach in Atlantic City and punched a police officer who had asked her to roll up her stockings.

Some young single **working-class** women, **middle-class** college students and free-spirited **upper-class** women decided to become flappers in the early 1920s. They challenged the traditional image of a woman by cutting their hair short, colouring it, putting on make-up and wearing short skirts with stockings rolled down to their knees. Once dressed for the evening, they drove themselves to clubs and dancehalls, where they smoked and danced the night away. These actions were a rejection of the values of their parents, who had grown up in the clean-living culture of the 19th century.

SOURCE F

An advert from 1928 in a mail order catalogue for a hat inspired by the flapper style. It is modelled by Clara Bow, the 'It Girl'.

Flappers also helped to change the position of women, because they challenged traditional attitudes. Some, like Clara Bow, who was known as the 'It Girl', became role models for young women. They felt more able to behave independently, which led to:

- more women going on dates without chaperones
- greater emphasis on appearance, with more money spent on perfume and make-up
- an increase in the number of women who had sex before marriage.

However, the flapper lifestyle was only for those who could afford it, which left out many **ethnic** and racial minority groups, and it was short-lived. Many flappers, as they aged, gave up their freedom and followed the more traditional pattern of getting married and having children.

SOURCE G

From an article about flappers in a US newspaper published in 1925, with the title 'Flapper Jane'.

"Jane, why do all of you dress the way you do?"

"In a way," says Jane, "it's just honesty. Women have come down off the pedestal lately. They are tired of this mysterious feminine-charm stuff. Maybe it goes with independence, earning your own living and voting and all that. Lots of them prefer to earn their own living and avoid the home-and-baby act. Well, anyhow, put it off for years and years."

EXAM-STYLE QUESTION

AO3   **AO4**

SKILLS CRITICAL THINKING, REASONING, DECISION MAKING, ADAPTIVE LEARNING, CREATIVITY, INNOVATION

Study Extract A.
Extract A suggests that the social restrictions women had faced before the war had weakened.
How far do you agree with this interpretation?
Use Extract A, Sources E and G and your own knowledge to explain your answer.   **(16 marks)**

HINT

This question targets your ability to use source material and your own knowledge to evaluate an historical interpretation.

ACTIVITY

1 Look at Source F. Write a brief that the designer might have used when they created the advert. Include:
   - the target audience for the advert
   - the methods used to make the product look appealing
   - a way the product could make women feel their position in society has improved.
2 Create an advert for an alternative product available in the 1920s that would appeal to women. It should show how the product would make women feel like they had more freedom.
3 Swap your advert with a partner. Repeat Question 1 with their advert.

1.5 PROBLEM INDUSTRIES

LEARNING OBJECTIVES

- Understand the reasons that farmers experienced problems in the 1920s, including over-production and mechanisation
- Understand the consequences of agricultural problems for farmers in the 1920s
- Understand the causes and effects of the decline of the older industries, including coal mining, textiles production and railroad transportation.

The 1920s was a decade of division. While many newer industries were successful, for those involved in farming, coal mining and textile manufacturing it was a difficult time.

> **KEY TERM**
>
> bushel a measurement used for crops including wheat and corn, equivalent to about 32 litres

Around one-third of the labour force in the USA worked on farms. During the First World War, they benefited from huge price rises. However, in the 1920s prices fell just as quickly. Wheat went from a high point of $2.50 per **bushel** to less than $1 per bushel, while cotton prices fell by as much as two-thirds. Farm incomes dropped and around two-thirds of farmers began to operate at a loss. They could no longer afford to pay their costs and, in 1924 alone, around 600,000 people lost their farms. Why was this?

CAUSES: OVER-PRODUCTION AND MECHANISATION

> **KEY TERM**
>
> tariffs taxes on imported goods, often introduced to encourage people to buy produce from their own country

The problem farmers faced was that demand for their goods fell, at the same time as their production rates rose. There were a wide variety of causes for this fall in demand.

- New man-made materials, such as rayon, along with the fashion for shorter skirts, meant there was less demand for cotton.
- Prohibition, a ban on the production, sale and drinking of alcohol, began in 1917 and was properly introduced in 1920. This reduced the demand for wheat, which was used as part of the brewing process.
- Mechanisation involved the replacement of horses with tractors. Instead of food, farmers now needed fuel to run their farm.
- The US government introduced measures such as the Emergency Tariff Act of 1921 which put **tariffs** on goods from overseas coming into the country. This made them more expensive, so Americans bought home-produced goods. However, other countries placed similar tariffs on their imports from the USA, so American goods became harder to sell outside the country.
- The recovery of Europe by 1922 meant their farms were able to produce enough food for them to feed themselves, reducing demand for imported food from the USA.

SOURCE H

A photo from 1925 of a farmer ploughing a field using a Ford tractor.

ACTIVITY

1 Imagine you are the farmer pictured in Source H. In pairs, each of you should write one of the following:
  ■ a thought bubble describing what the farmer may have been thinking in 1917
  ■ a thought bubble describing what the farmer may have been thinking in 1925.

2 Share your idea with your partner. Discuss what the differences between your responses are.

3 In your pair, choose one of the eight bullet points listed on these pages that you think gives the most important reason for the difference in your responses. Be prepared to share your idea with the class.

Even though fewer people wanted to buy farm produce, the amount US farms produced grew rapidly in the 1920s. This was partly a result of the First World War, which encouraged farmers to increase production. However, there were other factors that affected it.

■ Easy access to credit: the Agricultural Credits Act of 1923 made it easier for farmers to borrow money in order to run and improve their farms.

■ Mechanisation: there were ten times as many tractors in 1920 than there had been in 1915. This speeded up food production and made it possible to farm more land with fewer people.

■ Other scientific advances: during the war, the government had encouraged farmers to use new seeds, fertilisers and pesticides to increase the amount of crops they could produce.

The effect of these changes was that even though demand dropped in the 1920s, farmers produced 9 per cent more. In some years, the results of this over-production were very damaging. For example, there was an especially big cotton crop in 1926, but little demand for so much cotton. Its price dropped and many farmers in the southern states of the USA went **bankrupt** and their workers lost their jobs. All these problems meant that by the end of the 1920s, farm workers now made up only a fifth of the labour force. Their number had been reduced by around 1 million in 10 years.

EXAM-STYLE QUESTION

A01

Describe **two** features of the problems faced by US farmers in the 1920s.

(6 marks)

> **HINT**
>
> This question targets your ability to demonstrate knowledge and understanding of the key features of the period you have studied.

THE DECLINE OF OLDER INDUSTRIES

As newer industries producing motor cars, refrigerators and radios boomed in the 1920s, older ones started to decline. They faced two main problems: lower demand for their goods and increased competition from products that could replace them.

COAL MINING

Coal mining, which produced fuel to heat homes and power machines, suffered considerably. In 1920, 568 million **tonnes** of coal had been mined, but this fell to 518 million tonnes in 1930, even though the population grew during this period. This was because oil began to replace coal as a means of heating homes. By 1929, 550,000 homes were heated by oil. Miners also faced competition from electricity and gas as alternative sources of power.

TEXTILES FACTORIES

During the period before the war, the cotton and woollen mills had processed the material needed for clothing Americans. Afterwards, the textiles industry faced a huge drop in the demand for its goods due to changing fashions and competition from silk and the new material, rayon. As a result, textile production began to decline in the mills of New England, the Appalachian regions and the rural South. This was a problem the mill workers shared with the cotton farmers of the southern states of the USA, who struggled to find a market for their crop.

RAILROAD INDUSTRY

Another industry to suffer during the 1920s was the railroad industry. It had grown rapidly during the First World War to meet the need to transport supplies and troops around the USA. For example, the Railroad Administration had introduced a standard size for the track, speeding up transportation times. Progress did continue in the 1920s, as railroad use for the transportation of goods grew at a rate of around 10 per cent, but this was nowhere near the dramatic growth it had experienced in the late 19th and early 20th centuries. This had been slowed by the rise in car ownership for personal use, which affected passenger numbers on trains, and the increase in the number of roads, which meant more commercial goods were transported on them.

EFFECTS OF DECLINE

As the older industries declined, the workers suffered. It was not easy to find alternative work, because one industry often dominated a region. To do so, workers would have to leave their homes, find enough money to move to a new area and continue to support their family, without the guarantee of a new job. They would also have to overcome the challenge that they lacked the skills required for the new manufacturing industries, making them less attractive to employers. The result, illustrated by the various problems outlined in Figure 1.7, was that workers stayed in the older industries and experienced poverty.

ACTIVITY

1 Create a table with three headings: 'Causes', 'Key features' and 'Consequences'.
2 Sort the information on pages 20–23 into the table. Each row should be about one industry.
3 Challenge a partner by covering up one column of the table. They should try and guess what you have written in the column. Swap roles and repeat with a different column.

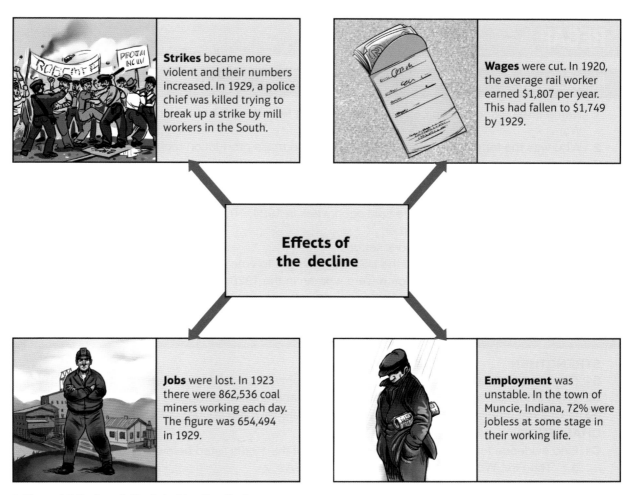

Strikes became more violent and their numbers increased. In 1929, a police chief was killed trying to break up a strike by mill workers in the South.

Wages were cut. In 1920, the average rail worker earned $1,807 per year. This had fallen to $1,749 by 1929.

Effects of the decline

Jobs were lost. In 1923 there were 862,536 coal miners working each day. The figure was 654,494 in 1929.

Employment was unstable. In the town of Muncie, Indiana, 72% were jobless at some stage in their working life.

▲ **Figure 1.7** Decline of older industries: the effects

SOURCE I

From an article in the *New York Daily News* by a reporter in the 1920s.

I have just returned from a visit to "Hell-in-Pennsylvania." I have seen horrible things there. Many times it seemed impossible to think we were in modern, civilized America. We saw thousands of women and children, literally starving to death. We found hundreds of destitute families living in crudely constructed bare-board shacks. They had been evicted from their homes by the coal companies.

SOURCE J

From a book by a French writer published in 1927, with the title *America comes of Age*.

European luxuries are often necessities in America. One could feed a whole country in Europe on what America wastes. American ideas of extravagance, comfort and sensible spending are entirely different from European. In America the daily life of the majority is on a scale that is reserved for the rich anywhere else. To the American, Europe is a land of poor people.

ACTIVITY

Can you explain why Sources I and J say such different things about America in the 1920s?

RECAP

RECALL QUIZ

1 Name three natural resources that were required from the USA to help defeat Germany during the First World War.
2 Who was the famous car manufacturer who used mass production techniques in the 1920s?
3 How much was spent on advertising in 1929: $1 billion, $2 billion or $5 billion?
4 Name two reasons that farmers over-produced wheat in the 1920s.
5 What replaced coal as a means of heating homes in the 1920s?
6 How many cinema tickets were sold each week in 1924: 10 million, 40 million or 75 million?
7 Name one famous jazz performer.
8 When was the first radio network set up?
9 When did women from across the USA get the right to vote?
10 What percentage of the workforce were women in the 1920s: 10 per cent, 20 per cent or 50 per cent?

CHECKPOINT

STRENGTHEN

S1 Describe, in detail, three reasons why the economy of the USA grew between 1918 and 1929.
S2 What evidence can you find that farmers and manufacturers struggled in the 1920s?
S3 Give three detailed examples of changes in the society and culture of the USA in the 1920s.

CHALLENGE

C1 Find evidence for each of the **interpretations** of the 1920s listed below:
    a 'The First World War helped improve the USA.'
    b 'There was a huge amount of social change in the 1920s.'
    c 'Most Americans benefited from the economic boom of the 1920s.'
C2 Find evidence to challenge each of the interpretations offered in **C1**.
C3 In your own words, write a summary of the USA in the 1920s, using the interpretations to provide a structure for your response.

How confident do you feel about your answers to these questions? If you're not sure you answered them well, create a table with two columns: 'Positive developments in the 1920s' and 'Negative developments in the 1920s'. Then use the material in the chapter to add notes to your table.

SUMMARY

- The First World War created demand for industrial and agricultural goods from the USA.
- There was an economic boom in the 1920s, because of mass production, hire purchase plans and advertising.
- Trading in stocks and shares became popular in the 1920s.
- An economic boom helped the leisure industry to grow, as people spent money on visits to cinemas, dance halls, jazz performances and sporting events.
- Advertising encouraged Americans to buy radio sets, cars and other consumer goods.
- Women's rights improved after the First World War, as more women joined the workforce and gained the right to vote.
- Some women rejected the values of their parents and became flappers.
- Coal mining, textiles production and the railroad industries all experienced decline in the 1920s.
- Over-production and a decline in demand created problems for American farmers.

EXAM GUIDANCE: PART (A) QUESTIONS

A01

Question to be answered: Describe two features of the leisure industry in the 1920s
(6 marks)

1 **Analysis Question 1: What is the question type testing?**
In this question you have to demonstrate that you have knowledge and understanding of the key features and characteristics of the period studied. In this particular case it is knowledge and understanding of the leisure industry in the 1920s.

2 **Analysis Question 2: What do I have to do to answer the question well?**
Obviously you have to write about the leisure industry! But it isn't just a case of writing everything you know. You have to write about two features. What are features? They are 'aspects' or 'characteristics'. We might even say that if you were allowed to put sub-headings in your answers, both features would be the sub-headings you would put.

So in this case you need to think about things linked to the leisure industry which you could write about. There are many of these. You could write about how baseball was so popular in the 1920s or how the popularity of other sports grew. There is plenty of material you could include on jazz and dancing, with reference to great musicians like Louis Armstrong. The boom in the cinema was very important at this time and the development of the motor car meant people could go and visit places that previously were too far away.

3 **Analysis Question 3: Are there any techniques I can use to make it very clear that I am doing what is needed to be successful?**
This is a 6-mark question and you need to make sure you leave enough time to answer the other two questions fully (they are worth 24 marks in total). Therefore you need to get straight in to writing your answer. The question asks for two features, so it's a good idea to write two paragraphs and to begin each paragraph with phrases like 'One feature was…', 'Another feature was…'. You will get a mark for each feature you identify and up to 2 marks for giving detail to support it. This gives the maximum of 6 marks.

You have to demonstrate knowledge, so make sure you back up your paragraphs with as much detailed knowledge as you have. But remember you are not writing an essay here. You are providing enough detail to pick up 2 extra marks on each feature you have identified.

Answer A

Leisure means what people do for fun in their spare time. Some people listened to the radio. Other people went to the cinema to see films.

What are the strengths and weaknesses of Answer A?
It doesn't have many strengths. It identifies a feature (what the leisure industry was) but the support that people listened to the radio is a bit obvious to count as detailed support. Other people went to the cinema might be another feature or it might be a bit of support for the first feature.

Whatever the examiners decide, this answer is not going to get more than 2 marks. It needs much more detail.

Answer B

One feature of the leisure industry was that people had more spare time, which they used to relax and enjoy themselves. Lots of Americans bought their own radio sets and listened to them in their homes. By 1929, 10 million sets had been sold. However, this also meant Americans listened to more adverts, which were broadcast on the radio.

An important feature of the leisure industry at this time was the growth of the film industry. Many people went to the cinema to watch films. These became more popular when colour was introduced in 1922, which was followed by sound in 1927. The popularity of films helped to create celebrities like Charlie Chaplin and Rudolph Valentino. Although people did not have televisions in their houses at this time, huge numbers of people saw films regularly at their local cinema. In 1924 around 40 million cinema tickets were sold each week. By 1929 this number had doubled.

What are the strengths and weaknesses of Answer B?
This is an excellent answer. It identifies two features (radio and cinema) and provides detailed support for them both.

There is no need to look for ways to improve this answer, you should just learn from it.

Challenge a friend
Use the Student Book to set a part (a) question for a friend. Then look at the answer. Does it do the following things?

☐ Identify two features
☐ Make it clear two features are being addressed
☐ Provide 3–4 lines of detailed information to support the feature.

If it does, you can tell your friend that the answer is very good!

2. INCREASED SOCIAL TENSIONS IN THE 1920S

LEARNING OBJECTIVES

- Understand the effects of attitudes and policies towards immigration
- Understand the impact of racist attitudes towards black Americans and the return of the Ku Klux Klan
- Understand the key features of the Prohibition era and the growth of organised crime.

If you were white, had a north-western European cultural background, followed the Protestant religion and did not want to drink alcohol, life in the 1920s would have suited you. However, if you did not fit this description, you could face persecution for your ethnic background, arrest for your political values and intolerance of your religious beliefs and moral principles.

These challenges varied depending on who you were. For potential immigrants, the biggest barrier was getting into the USA as government policy became more restrictive. For those people who did get in, there was a suspicious government to worry about, which assumed most immigrants were trying to start a revolution. For those people who already lived in the USA, there were racist organisations that harassed black people, fundamentalist Christians who tried to stop the teaching of modern science and gangsters who took over entire cities.

2.1 ATTITUDES AND POLICIES TOWARDS IMMIGRATION

LEARNING OBJECTIVES

- Understand how attitudes towards immigration changed
- Understand what policies were introduced concerning immigration
- Understand the impact of those policies.

ATTITUDES

Until the early years of the 20th century, the USA had happily accepted immigrants from around the world. They provided a cheap source of **labour** both for farmers and factory owners. However, after the First World War attitudes began to change.

Traditionally, most immigrants had come from western Europe and formed the largest ethnic grouping in the USA – the White Anglo-Saxon Protestants (WASPS). However, in the decade before the war the majority of immigrants had come from countries such as Italy, Austria–Hungary, Russia, Western Poland and Greece, in eastern and southern Europe. This wave of immigration upset some Americans because:

- Many of the immigrants were Catholics or Jews and so had a different cultural and religious background to the majority of the people already in the country.
- The immigrants were often poor, illiterate and could not speak English.
- There was a fear that some of the immigrants brought with them undemocratic ideas and supported **radicalism**. Fear of communism was particularly strong after the Russian Revolution in 1917.
- Many American workers were worried that workers from other countries would accept lower wages and take their jobs from them.

KEY TERM

radicalism the desire for dramatic social change

EXTEND YOUR KNOWLEDGE

HARRY LAUGHLIN

Harry Laughlin was an educator and sociologist who believed that people from southern and eastern Europe were born inferior. His research suggested they were more likely to end up in a prison or mental hospital than other ethnic groups. In 1922, he published a book that promoted their forced sterilisation in order to prevent them from having children. Several states made this into law, carrying it out on a small scale and there were people in the federal government who sympathised with his views. The Secretary of Labor sent Laughlin to Europe in 1923 to investigate nations that sent people to the USA. Congress then used his conclusions to create new immigration laws.

SOURCE A

A US banking poster from the 1920s. It shows an immigrant family arriving in the USA.

They Win Citizenship, Contentment, Riches, by Loyalty, Industry and Thrift

SOURCE B

From a speech by Senator Ellison Smith of South Carolina, given in April 1924 to Congress.

I think we now have enough people in our country for us to shut the door and to breed up a pure American citizenship. I would make this not an escape for the oppressed of all countries, but a country to develop that splendid type of man that has made America the best nation in her progress and in her power.

POLICIES

The USA passed two new laws in the 1920s to restrict immigration. The first piece of **legislation**, the Emergency Quota Act of 1921, limited immigration numbers from outside the western half of the world to 357,000 per year. It also tried to maintain the ethnic mix of the US population by controlling the number of people that could come from each country. Each country could send 3 per cent of the number of people from their nation living in the USA in 1920. This gave an advantage to groups who had been in the USA for a longer period of time, so had larger numbers and had become well-established. This was mainly those from western Europe and discriminated against those from southern and eastern Europe.

The law became even more restrictive in 1924, when the National Origins Act was passed. It was designed to try and further reduce the number of people from southern and eastern European backgrounds in the USA. The new law lowered the quota from 357,000 to around 164,000 immigrants per year. According to the law, each country could now send 2 per cent of the number of people from their nation living in the USA in 1890. There were far fewer people from southern and eastern Europe in the USA in 1890, which meant very few were allowed in. In 1929, the quota was reduced again to 150,000, but still allowed for immigration from the Americas.

SOURCE C

From a speech by Congressman London, given to Congress in April 1921.

To prevent immigration means to cripple the United States. Our most developed industrial states are those which have had the largest immigration. Our most backward states industrially and educationally are those which had little immigration. By this bill to restrict immigration we, who have escaped the horrors of the First World War, will refuse a place of safety to the victims of the war.

EXAM-STYLE QUESTION

A03

SKILLS ANALYSIS, ADAPTIVE LEARNING, CREATIVITY

Study Sources B and C.
How far does Source B support the evidence of Source C about immigration to the USA in the 1920s?
Explain your answer.   **(8 marks)**

HINT

This question targets your ability to comprehend, interpret and cross-refer sources.

IMPACT

The new laws transformed the US immigration system and numbers fell rapidly. In 1914, around 1.2 million immigrants had arrived in the USA each year but, even with unrestricted immigration from Canada and Mexico, this had fallen to around 280,000 immigrants by 1929. The change in policy also led to new **enforcement** measures and a border patrol was set up in 1925 to try and prevent illegal immigration. In the course of a decade, the nation had changed from a welcoming 'open-door' country to a considerably more restrictive and less welcoming one.

ACTIVITY

1 Source A was designed to promote the idea of saving money. Discuss with a partner how this purpose affects the image it gives of immigrants.
2 Decide with your partner whether the designer of Source A would agree with the speaker in Source B or Source C. Be prepared to share your answer with the class.
3 Construct a table that summarises the changes in US immigration policy in 1921, 1924 and 1929.

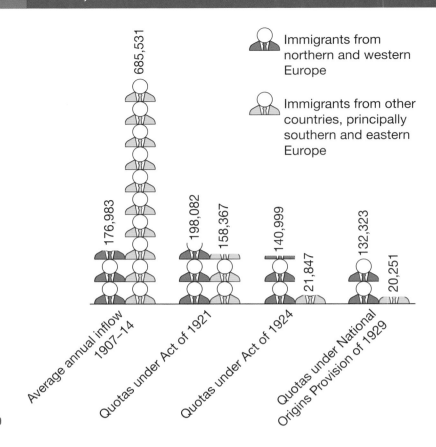

▶ **Figure 2.1** Sources of immigration 1907–29

2.2 THE PALMER RAIDS AND THE 'RED SCARE'

LEARNING OBJECTIVES

☐ Understand the causes of the 'Red Scare' and its influence

☐ Understand the key features of the Palmer Raids

☐ Understand the consequences of the 'Red Scare' and the Palmer Raids.

THE 'RED SCARE'

KEY TERMS

communism a way of organising society in which there is no private property and everything is shared

Soviet Union the name that Russia came to be known as from 1922

anarchist a person who rejects the idea of organised government

Many middle and upper-class Americans feared **communism**, because it threatened to transform society, taking away their wealth and power. However, it was not until 1917, when revolution took place in Russia, that the idea of a communist government became a reality. There was now a model that communists in other countries could follow in order to bring about their own revolution. Worldwide revolution was promoted by an organisation called Comintern in the **Soviet Union**. The US government were particularly concerned, because immigrants from eastern and southern Europe brought communist, as well as **anarchist**, ideas with them.

In 1919, these concerns were increased by an outbreak of **unrest** and anger amongst industrial workers, whose wages were low and rights were few. In total, there were around 3,600 strikes across the USA, including a general strike in Seattle of 100,000 workers and a police strike in Boston that created a serious challenge for law and order. This unsettled powerful American politicians and industrial bosses, whose safety was threatened by this unrest. In April 1919, 40 mail bombs addressed to important politicians and industrialists were found by the postal service. Then in June, eight cities experienced bomb attacks, including one outside the house of the attorney general, Alexander Palmer. This pushed Palmer and the government into action.

SOURCE D

A US cartoon from 1919 published during the 'Red Scare' and captioned 'Put Them Out and Keep Them Out'. It shows a communist setting the US flag on fire.

THE PALMER RAIDS

Attorney General Palmer's first measure was to set up the General Intelligence Division, headed by John Edgar Hoover, which later became a part of the Federal Bureau of Investigation (FBI). It was created in order to spy on, secretly join and then arrest the members of **radical** groups. They began to take action on 7 November 1919, when the offices of the Union of Russian Workers were searched and arrests were made. These **raids** continued into early 1920, reaching their peak on 2 January when raids took place in 33 cities on any group Palmer and Hoover believed to be radical.

CONSEQUENCES

During the Palmer Raids, thousands of arrests were made and around 600 radicals were **deported** from the USA. Although most of those arrested were later released, the conditions they were kept in were very bad. For example, on Deer Island, where Boston's radicals were held, prisoners died from the extreme cold and one felt so desperate he committed suicide. The effects of the scare and raids were also felt in the longer term, as they:

- increased support for restrictions on immigration, because it was believed that many immigrants supported radical ideas
- weakened the trade union movement, because some of their members were communists and they had organised the strikes of 1919.

By mid-1920, the situation had begun to calm down. After the first raids, Palmer had tried to stir up more fear as part of his plan to stand for the presidency. He claimed that there would be an increase in the level of communist protest and violence on May Day 1920, but the day came and went without violence. After that, his reputation was destroyed and the 'Red Scare' died out.

ACTIVITY

1 Write down the message of Source D, using detail from the cartoon to explain how the cartoonist communicates this message.
2 Create an alternative caption for Source D. Share your idea with a partner and decide if they both have the same message.
3 With your partner, split up the events of the 'Red Scare' and Palmer Raids into six stages. Make sure you include causes, events and consequences.
4 Design your own storyboard to illustrate each of the six stages.

EXAM-STYLE QUESTION

Describe **two** features of the 'Red Scare' (1919–20). **(6 marks)**

A01

HINT

This question targets your ability to demonstrate knowledge and understanding of the key features of the period you have studied.

2.3 THE SACCO AND VANZETTI CASE

LEARNING OBJECTIVES

- Understand the crime of which Sacco and Vanzetti were accused
- Understand the evidence that was discussed at their trial
- Understand the outcome and international impact of their trial.

THE ROBBERY

At 3.00 p.m. on 15 April 1920, two Italian immigrants committed an armed robbery in Braintree, Massachusetts. They shot the paymaster and a guard at a shoe factory, stealing $15,776.51 and escaping before anyone could stop them. A police investigation began immediately, but it took several weeks before any leads were found.

Then, in early May, the police heard that a car associated with the crime had been taken to a local garage. The mechanic was told to call the police when it was collected. On the night of 5 May 1920, two Italians, one a shoe factory worker called Nicola Sacco and the other a fish salesman called Bartolomeo

Vanzetti, came to pick up the car. The mechanic's wife tried to stall them while the police were contacted, but the pair became very nervous and left. The police caught up with them and they were arrested. They were both carrying guns.

Sacco and Vanzetti, who were both anarchists, believed they had been arrested because of their connection to the 1919 'Red Scare' bombings. As a result, they lied to the police about their beliefs, the people they knew and where they had been on the day of the shooting. Soon, however, their link to the anarchist movement was discovered. This information greatly reduced their chances of getting a fair trial, as many Americans were both anti-immigrant and anti-anarchist. The people who would sit on the jury and decide their guilt were likely to be unsympathetic to Sacco and Vanzetti.

THE TRIAL

It took a year before the trial was held, but in May 1921, a jury of 12 men prepared to listen to the evidence of 167 witnesses. A summary of what they were asked to consider by Judge Webster Thayer is given in Figure 2.2.

Guilty?

The gun: a ballistics expert believed that the bullet could have been fired from Sacco's gun.

Their background: Vanzetti had a previous conviction for armed robbery and they were both draft-dodgers and anarchists.

The lies: both men lied to police after their arrest.

Eyewitnesses: the prosecution was able to find lots of eyewitnesses to the crime and some identified Sacco and Vanzetti.

Innocent?

The gun: the evidence was tampered with in a later trial and the expert's evidence was not conclusive.

Their background: character witnesses, including Sacco's boss and two policemen, said that they had a good reputation.

The lies: they thought the investigation was connected to the 'Red Scare' bombings, which they had links to, and so they lied.

Eyewitnesses: both had alibis. Six people saw Vanzetti selling fish in Plymouth and Sacco was seen at the Italian consulate.

▲ **Figure 2.2** The trial of Sacco and Vanzetti

EXTEND YOUR KNOWLEDGE

FINDING A JURY

The first jurors who were called to the courtroom were worried that they would be attacked by Sacco and Vanzetti's supporters. As a result, they all found reasons to be excused. In fact, over 500 potential jurors found reasons to escape service, including one who claimed to be deaf but then answered the questions put to him. In the end, the judge had to order people from outside the courtroom to be interviewed until 12 eligible jurors were found.

THE RESULTS

The jury was asked to make its decision on 14 July 1921, and it was made before the day was over. At 7.55 p.m. the court heard the judgment. Sacco and Vanzetti were found guilty and sentenced to death by **electrocution**. However, the pair's supporters believed this was an unfair decision, especially as Judge Thayer was a known anti-anarchist and clearly sided against them. Appeals followed, but all without success. The trial had shown that, even without conclusive evidence, two immigrants from southern Europe could be found guilty of a crime and sentenced to death.

Despite the failure of Sacco and Vanzetti's defence, it did cause some people to challenge the US anti-immigrant position.
- It led to protests around the world: workers protested in 60 cities in Italy, as well as in other parts of the world, and a mail bomb was sent to the American embassy in Paris on 19 October 1921.
- It united immigrants in the USA: the Sacco-Vanzetti Defense Committee was set up on 9 May 1920. It managed to raise around $300,000 to support the defence of Sacco and Vanzetti.

THE EXECUTION

EXTRACT A

From a history of the USA, published in 2013.

Each side accused the other of persuading people to be 'eyewitnesses'. There was no clear evidence. However, the judge at the trial made it clear that he expected a 'guilty' verdict. He got one. There were appeals, petitions and protests, in the USA and abroad. The men were finally executed on 23 August 1927.

The two men were executed in 1927, but their story was not forgotten. Fifty years later many Americans were convinced that they had been found guilty because of their nationality and political beliefs, rather than because of any evidence against them. Although the governor of Massachusetts refused to pardon them, he did agree to make 23 August 1977 the 'Nicola Sacco and Bartolomeo Vanzetti Memorial Day'. Whether they were guilty or not he could not say, but he was certain they had been denied a fair trial. Even today, the question of their guilt is still subject to debate.

ACTIVITY

1 Study Extract A. Write down one fact the historian uses and find one piece of evidence from pages 32–34 to support it.
2 Pick one opinion the historian offers. Write it down and find three pieces of evidence to support it and one to challenge it.
3 Write a short speech calling for a re-trial. Read it out to a partner and ask them to sum up your argument in one sentence.

2.4 ATTITUDES TOWARDS BLACK AMERICANS

LEARNING OBJECTIVES

- Understand the reasons for racist attitudes in the USA
- Understand how black Americans were treated across the USA
- Understand the effect of racist attitudes on the lives of black Americans.

BACKGROUND

In 1918 many black Americans were victims of **discrimination**. Although slavery had been brought to an end after the American Civil War (1861–65), this did not mean that black Americans had achieved equality.

TREATMENT IN THE SOUTH

The white Americans who governed the South had looked for ways to keep
black Americans separate from white Americans and restrict their position
in society. They passed a series of laws, together known as the **Jim Crow
laws** to segregate society. So in 1918 black people still sat in different parts
of restaurants, travelled on different railway carriages and used different
toilets. Their educational opportunities were limited by the availability of
black schools, which meant that only around 1 per cent of black people
of high school age were able to attend one. Some protested to the federal
government, but even the Supreme Court refused to challenge the Jim Crow
laws.

Without government support, black southerners felt powerless. The
government did little to protect them, which meant their lives were at risk from
racist violence. In its worst form, this involved a lynch mob that would **kidnap**
the person they thought was guilty of a crime, beat him and then hang or burn
him without a trial. The police rarely stopped these lynchings and are known
to have sometimes taken part. For example, in June 1919, Jackson's local
newspaper reported that a black man arrested for rape was to be released by
the police, who expected that a mob would then kidnap and burn him. Events
like this happened across the USA, but most were concentrated in the South
and their number remained high. Even after 400,000 black people had served
in the First World War, 76 were lynched in 1919.

SOURCE E

A photo from 1925 of a lynch mob in Missouri. It shows a black American (behind the
branches) being lynched.

THE GREAT MIGRATION TO THE NORTH

The northern states of the USA had not seen large numbers of slaves working in agriculture and so for many northerners, their experience of black people came largely as a result of the Great Migration of black people from the South that began during the First World War. Around 1.5 million black people migrated to northern cities to escape racism and to find employment in factories. However, they did not find equality in the North. Most had unskilled jobs, earning low wages, which meant they lived in large **ghettos** in poor quality houses. For example, the black population of Harlem, in New York City, rose from 50,000 in 1919 to 165,000 by 1930. In effect, this meant black people were segregated by their lack of wealth.

Another problem black people faced was the anger of white industrial workers, whose jobs the black migrants competed for. This sometimes turned into violent race riots (see Chapter 1, page 7), which reached their peak shortly after the First World War. The combination of reduced demand for goods produced by the older industries and the high number of soldiers returning to their old factory jobs created the atmosphere for the race riots. In 1919, 24 locations across the USA experienced riots. Even after the riots began to decline in number, many white northerners now shared similar attitudes to those in the South.

IMPACT OF RACIST ATTITUDES

EXTEND YOUR KNOWLEDGE

LITERACY TESTS
Literacy tests were first used in the state of Connecticut in 1855 to stop Irish immigrants voting. Southern states adopted these tests in the late 19th century to restrict the voting rights of black Americans. Often, white Americans who had poor reading and writing abilities were not required to take the tests.

Racism throughout the USA created a wide range of difficulties for black people. It affected their:

- Job opportunities: the lack of good quality education meant that most black people were forced into unskilled factory work, farm labour or domestic service.
- Job security: black people were the most likely to lose their jobs when the economy struggled. For example, many black farm workers lost their jobs in the 1920s.
- Living conditions and facilities: houses in the South lacked basic plumbing and electricity. Segregated facilities were usually of lower quality too.
- Right to vote: southerners tried to stop black people voting, forcing them to take literacy tests from which white people were exempt.

ACTIVITY

1 Create a set of cards with the following titles: 'Slavery', 'Jim Crow law', 'Lynching', 'Race riots', 'Great Migration', 'Ghettos', 'Lack of opportunities', 'Poor conditions' and 'Voting restrictions'.
2 Add some detail about each topic onto the back of the cards.
3 Combine your set of cards with a partner so that there are 18 cards. Take it in turns to pick up two cards and make a link between them. If successful, the player keeps the cards. Repeat until you can no longer make links with the remaining cards. The winner is the player with the most cards in their pile.

2.5 THE KU KLUX KLAN

LEARNING OBJECTIVES

- ■ Understand the values and structure of the Ku Klux Klan
- ■ Understand the methods used by the Ku Klux Klan to persecute black people
- ■ Understand the impact of the Ku Klux Klan on the US government and legal system.

THE ORGANISATION OF THE KU KLUX KLAN

KEY TERM

bootlegger someone who smuggles alcohol

EXTEND YOU KNOWLEDGE

KLANSPEAK

Leaders of the KKK wanted to make their members feel like they were in an exclusive club. In order to create this atmosphere, they used made-up terms that only Klansmen fully understood. Their local group was called a Klavern, which was led by a Kleagle, who reported to a Klud. Their ultimate leader was called the Imperial Wizard, who set out the rituals they should follow in the Kloran. Even the name of the group itself, which came from the Greek word for circle (kýklos), gave it a mysterious feel.

The original Ku Klux Klan (KKK) formed after the American Civil War to defend white **supremacy** over black people. Its members attacked and intimidated black people because they did not want them to vote or have their own politicians. Their violence reached such heights that they were shut down in 1871 by the federal government, but underground groups continued to work for white supremacy. Influenced by the 1915 film *Birth of a Nation*, which showed the Klan as heroes and black people as evil, William Simmons, an insurance salesman, restarted the organisation and worked hard to boost its membership.

Under Simmons, the new KKK still fought for white supremacy, but he expanded its core values. These were:
- ■ that white Anglo-Saxon Protestants (WASPs) were a superior race of people, who needed to fight to survive
- ■ that immigration should stop, because it brought foreigners into the USA who threatened the power of WASPs
- ■ that WASPs should have strong Christian values. The Klan targeted criminals who did not meet their moral standards, such as **adulterers** and **bootleggers**.

In order to put these values into practice, Simmons also gave the Klan a modern organisation structure. It was divided into chapters, or Klaverns, and each Klansman reported to their local leader, or Kleagle. With this clearly defined structure, Simmons was able to spread the Klan outside the South and across the USA.

MEMBERSHIP

In the 1920s, membership numbers for the Klan rose quickly, mainly because Simmons recruited two public relations experts to help him. These were Edward Clarke and Elizabeth Tyler, who came up with new ways to attract members. For example, they allowed Kleagles to keep $4 from the $10 joining fee, which encouraged them to recruit members. As a result, by 1923, the Klan had 5 million members spread across 4,000 chapters. These were mainly people from the urban middle class, like small businessmen and some professionals, who wanted to force their own values on others.

METHODS

The Klan used a variety of methods to persecute black people, protect white supremacy and stop others from breaking their moral code (see Figure 2.3).

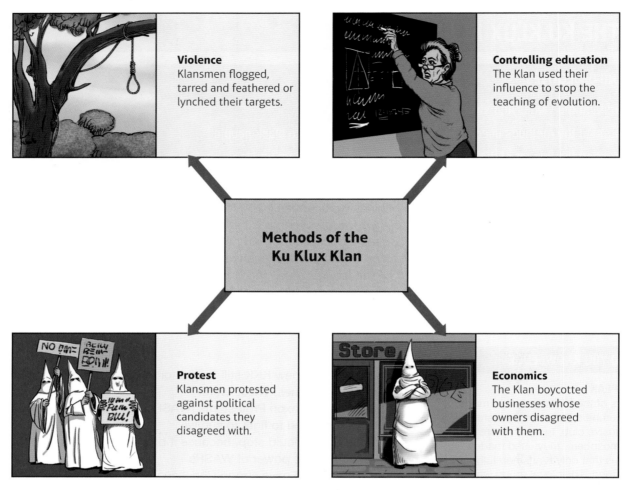

▲ **Figure 2.3** Methods of the Ku Klux Klan

At its height in the mid-1920s, the KKK had some very powerful members from all over the USA. These included senators from Texas and Indiana, the governor of Alabama and the mayor of Portland in Oregon, which gave the Klan considerable political power. They also had influence over the legal system, because some judges and police officers were members, or were sympathetic to the Klan, making it difficult for victims of Klansmen to get equality before the law.

However, this situation did not last for long and the Klan's power began to decline after 1925. In that year, an influential Grand Dragon (state leader), called David Stephenson, was found guilty of the rape and murder of a 28-year-old woman. This damaged the reputation of the Klan and membership numbers fell. By 1929, there were only around 200,000 members left.

SOURCE F

From an article by Hiriam Wesley Evans, the Klan's Imperial Wizard, 1926, about the treatment of white Anglo-Saxon Protestants in the USA.

The Klan has come to speak for most Americans of the old pioneer stock. The Nordic (WASP) American today is a stranger in large parts of the land his fathers gave him. Moreover, he is a most unwelcome stranger, one much spit upon, and one to whom even the right to have his own opinions and to work for his own interests is now denied with insults and abuse.

ACTIVITY

Read pages 37–39 and make notes on the KKK in a table using the following headings:
- values
- reasons why they attracted more members after 1915
- impact on US society.

EXAM-STYLE QUESTION

A03

SKILLS ANALYSIS, ADAPTIVE LEARNING, CREATIVITY

SOURCE G

From an article by Robert Doffus about the KKK in a US magazine published in 1923, with the title *How the Ku Klux Klan Sells Hate*.

The organization caught good citizens as well as bad and indifferent ones. They found that sometimes getting out of the Klan was not so simple as getting in. Merchants were afraid to drop out because of boycotts, politicians because they feared to lose votes, editors because they dared not risk offending readers and advertisers. Often men were threatened with bodily harm, either for refusing to join or for trying to withdraw.

Study Sources F and G.
How far does Source F support the evidence of Source G about the reason some Americans might have supported the Ku Klux Klan in the 1920s?
Explain your answer.   **(8 marks)**

HINT

This question targets your ability to comprehend, interpret and cross-refer sources.

2.6 MORALS, VALUES AND THE 'MONKEY TRIAL'

LEARNING OBJECTIVES

- Understand the debate between modernists and fundamentalists
- Understand the key features of the 'Monkey Trial'
- Understand the national consequences of the 'Monkey Trial'.

MORALS AND VALUES

The USA was home to a range of religions, but most Americans were Protestant. In the 19th century, this group had begun to divide into **fundamentalists** and modernists. Fundamentalists believed that everything in the Bible had actually happened. For example, that Eve had been created from Adam's rib and a whale had swallowed Jonah. They had old-fashioned values and disliked activities like dancing and following the latest fashions.

Fundamentalists were most influential in the rural and small town communities of the **Bible Belt**, but they also had supporters in the cities. **Evangelist** Aimee Semple McPherson, for instance, was very popular and built a megachurch in Los Angeles that had a tank designed to **baptise** 150 people at once. She also used the radio to help spread Christian messages with fundamentalist themes promoting strict morals and traditional values.

In contrast to fundamentalists, modernists believed that as a result of modern scientific discoveries, Bible stories had to be reinterpreted. They believed that God was the ultimate creator, but felt that developments like the creation of the world were a bit more complex than the Bible stated. For example, modernists accepted **Darwinism**, while still believing that God was behind the **evolutionary** process. Modernists also argued that moral values could not remain the same for all of human history. Instead, they changed according to historical circumstances.

KEY TERMS

Bible Belt southern and mid-western states in the USA, where many people hold fundamentalist Christian beliefs

Darwinism the theory of evolution by natural selection developed by naturalist Charles Darwin and published in his book, *The Descent of Man* (1871)

THE ORIGINS OF THE 'MONKEY TRIAL'

The Anti-Evolution League of America was set up to campaign against the teaching of Darwin's theory of evolution in US schools. The League disagreed with Darwin's idea that man was related to monkeys. In 1925, their campaign succeeded in Tennessee, which passed the Butler Act, making it illegal to teach the theory of evolution in the state. Anyone found doing so could be fined up to $500. A few modernists in the small town of Dayton were very angry and approached John Scopes, a high school teacher, to volunteer to break the law to see if it would be enforceable in the courts. Scopes agreed, taught the theory and was arrested.

THE TRIAL

John Scopes' trial began on 10 July 1925. The **prosecution** was led by William Jennings-Bryan, a popular fundamentalist who had run for the presidency three times and campaigned for the anti-evolution law. He faced an equally well-known lawyer, Clarence Darrow, who led the defence. Darrow, an **agnostic**, was a member of the American Civil Liberties Union. As a result of their involvement, a small-town trial became a national event.

The trial itself began calmly. The prosecution called a number of witnesses who **testified** that Scopes had taught Darwinism. However, Darrow wanted to challenge the law itself and turn the trial into a debate between fundamentalist ideas like creationism and modernist ones like the theory of evolution. This is why it became known as the 'Monkey Trial'. In taking this approach, Darrow helped turn a routine trial into a dramatic courtroom battle, which, at its most entertaining, involved Bryan and Darrow talking over each other and shaking their fists in anger.

The cause of this moment of intense anger was a request, by Darrow, to put Bryan on the stand so that he could ask him about his beliefs. Opening with a question about whether Jonah was swallowed by a whale, then about the story of Noah and the Flood and finishing with an examination of how long it took God to create the world, Darrow tried to challenge the ideas of fundamentalism. Bryan, however, would not back down and defended the beliefs of his fellow fundamentalists. The examination ended with an attack, by Bryan, on Darrow's attitude to the Bible, while Darrow called Bryan's ideas foolish.

EXTEND YOUR KNOWLEDGE

CLARENCE DARROW

Clarence Darrow spent most of his early career as a lawyer defending causes that were important to him. He defended anarchists charged with murder in 1886, union leaders involved in a bombing in 1911 and war protestors charged with anti-government behaviour during the First World War. After this, he focused on criminal law. His most famous case, from 1924, involved teenage murderers Leopold and Loeb, who had killed for the thrill of it. He helped them escape the death penalty and get life imprisonment instead. Darrow's involvement in the murder case turned him into a national celebrity.

THE JUDGMENT

Darrow's case had tried to make the trial about ideas, rather than the actions of Scopes. However, the judge, who was a committed Protestant himself, refused to accept this. He said the question for the jury was whether Scopes had taught evolution. The jury agreed that he had and the fine was set at $100.

On the surface, the trial had achieved little. The Butler Act remained in force until 1967 and the Anti-Evolution League convinced more states to pass laws against teaching evolution in schools. Nevertheless, some progress was made by the modernists:
- The trial helped the religious debate get national attention: hundreds of reporters came to Dayton and the trial itself was the first to be reported word-for-word on national radio.
- It damaged the cause of fundamentalism: Bryan's fundamentalist beliefs were mocked by many national newspapers and urban audiences.

SOURCE H

A US magazine cover from 1925 about the 'Monkey Trial'. It shows a caricature of the prosecutor, William Jennings Bryan.

JULY 18, 1925   PRICE 15 CENT.

Judge

EVOLUTION NUMBER

PIN THE TAIL ON THE MONKEY

THE NEW GAME

Describe **two** features of the 'Monkey Trial'.   **(6 marks)**

A01

HINT

This question targets your ability to demonstrate knowledge and understanding of the key features of the period you have studied.

ACTIVITY

1 Discuss the message of Source H with a partner. Share your findings with the class.
2 Design your own magazine front cover giving a fundamentalist point of view about the 'Monkey Trial'.

2.7 PROHIBITION AND THE GANGSTERS

LEARNING OBJECTIVES

- ☐ Understand the reasons for the introduction of Prohibition in the USA
- ☐ Understand the positive and negative effects of Prohibition
- ☐ Understand the role of gangsters during the Prohibition era.

PROHIBITION

For at least a century, drinkers of alcohol (wets) and non-drinkers (drys) had argued over the right to drink alcohol. In 1919, this argument appeared to come to an end, when the Eighteenth Amendment of the US Constitution was introduced. This banned the manufacture, sale and transportation of alcoholic drinks. A year later, the Volstead Act was passed, which set up a system for enforcing the ban. The USA was now, in theory at least, a country in which it was impossible to consume alcohol.

CAUSES

KEY TERM

temperance abstinence from alcohol

During the 19th century, campaign groups from the **temperance** movement fought for the prohibition of alcohol. The Women's Christian Temperance Union, founded in 1874, used peaceful methods like marches to campaign against alcohol. Later, the Anti-Saloon League, set up in 1893, pressured the government directly to end the drinking of alcohol. Both groups used a variety of arguments, which included:

- Alcohol damaged society: women said that alcohol consumption affected family life because it led to unemployment, wages being wasted in the bar and domestic violence.
- It led to sinful behaviour: religious groups believed alcohol was responsible for sin.
- It weakened the economy: workers who were drunk, or recovering from drinking alcohol, were less efficient in their jobs.
- It created problems for a country at war: grain was needed for food production, rather than alcohol manufacture, during the First World War.

These arguments were highly effective and by 1917, around half the states of the USA had already passed prohibition laws. Two years later, the rest of the country joined the ban.

POSITIVE EFFECTS

In some ways, Prohibition was a success. Alcohol consumption dropped and the health of Americans improved. For example, the number of deaths from liver disease fell from 29.5 per 100,000 in 1911 to 10.7 in 1929. It was also a fairly popular measure, as a survey by a weekly magazine suggested that around 40 per cent of the population were in favour of enforcing the prohibition law.

SOURCE I

From an essay published in the USA in 1925, with the title *Prohibition as seen by a Business Man*.

Especially noteworthy have been the effects upon production. The efficiency of the average workers was increased. Instead of dulled minds, unsteady muscles and jumping nerves after the weekend, the workers began the week on Monday with full power.

Prohibition also created new markets for our products. Instead of beer, better homes, better furniture and better clothes were demanded. The great mass of the people are sober, making money, buying luxuries, banking undreamed sums and keeping business thriving.

This enforcement, carried out by prohibition agents, could be effective too. One famous partnership, Izzy Einstein and Moe Smith, seized around 5 million bottles of alcohol in the 1920s. This suggested, on the surface at least, that Prohibition was improving lives, well received and properly enforced.

NEGATIVE EFFECTS

The true picture, however, was quite different. As soon as Prohibition began, problems arose. Breweries who manufactured beer, the farmers who supplied them and the saloons who sold their products all suffered. Thousands of Americans lost their jobs, or part of their income, which meant they had less to spend on leisure activities and consumer goods. The ban also affected the government, because they lost income from the tax on alcohol. One anti-Prohibition group estimated this loss at $11 billion by 1931. These economic effects suggest that Prohibition actually harmed the US economy.

KEY TERMS

speakeasies a slang word for places, usually shops, clubs or bars, where alcohol could be bought illegally

moonshine an alcoholic drink that has been made illegally, sometimes used to refer to smuggled alcohol too

Prohibition also created enforcement problems, turning some Americans into criminals. In order to get access to illegal alcohol, people were prepared to:
- smuggle alcoholic drinks, like Canadian whiskey and Mexican tequila, into the USA
- try and turn industrial or medicinal alcohol into something drinkable
- visit **speakeasies** to purchase illegal drinks
- make their own homemade **moonshine**.

As a result, drinking alcohol became an underground activity, hidden from law enforcement officers. While this meant Americans could continue drinking, it also put their lives at risk from poor quality moonshine. For example, in New York City, 34 people died from wood alcohol poisoning over 4 days.

SOURCE J

From the notes of Jane Addams, a social worker, written in the 1920s during the Prohibition era.

The alcohol is moved sometimes in an old grocery wagon, sometimes in a motor truck. The residents of a street near the house were used to seeing a man sitting on a front seat beside the driver of an old Ford truck with a shotgun wrapped in newspaper lying across his knee. This was to protect the bootleggers from hijackers or policemen. Our neighbourhood was filled with bootleggers, coming from various parts of the city.

Poor enforcement of the prohibition law was at the root of these problems. An enforcement division had been set up in the US Treasury Department, but at first it was only given $2 million to stop the bootleggers, alcohol manufacturers and speakeasy owners. This problem was made worse by opposition from five states that refused to enforce Prohibition, and American juries, which refused to convict law breakers. As a consequence, out of 6,904 Prohibition cases between 1921 and 1924 in New York, only 20 people were convicted. Despite its good intentions, it was clear that Prohibition was not as popular as the campaign groups had assumed it would be.

SOURCE K

A photo of a man producing moonshine in the 1920s. It shows the equipment required to break the prohibition law.

THE GANGSTERS

Prohibition provided an opportunity for organised crime to grow in the 1920s. It was clear that ordinary people wanted to drink alcohol, providing a market for gangs who could produce, smuggle and sell it to them. In some cities, like Chicago and New York, these gangs grew larger as they made money from businesses associated with drinking. Gang bosses ran gambling dens and brothels, co-ordinated **loan sharks** and made local businesses pay protection money to them.

One of the most successful bosses was Al Capone. Based in Chicago, he began his criminal career as a manager at a speakeasy called the Four Deuces, working for a gang boss called Jonny Torrio. Capone impressed his boss by helping to protect the Chicago Outfit gang's interests across the city. As a consequence, by the time Capone was 25, Torrio had retired and Capone took over control of the gang.

At the height of his power, Capone earned around $105 million a year from organised crime. However, his profits were always at risk from competing gangs who wanted to take over his territory. This meant he had to use extreme violence to protect it. For example, on Valentine's Day 1929, Capone's men, dressed as policemen, tried to kill Bugs Moran, the leader of the rival North Side gang. Although Moran escaped the ambush, seven of his men were lined up and shot dead, showing the cruelty with which Capone maintained his territory.

Actions like this continued until the federal government decided to take action. First, Eliot Ness, a prohibition agent, put together a team to target Capone. His team, known as the Untouchables, raided warehouses and seized illegal alcohol. This made it more difficult for Capone to maintain his control of

EXTEND YOUR KNOWLEDGE

THE TREATMENT OF TRAITORS
If someone betrayed Al Capone, they could expect a horrible fate. One member of his gang, John Scalise, was planning to assassinate him. When Capone heard this, he took decisive action. Scalise, along with two of his allies, were invited to a party. They were given food and treated well. Then, after dinner, the mood changed. Capone accused them of disloyalty. The traitors were tied up and Capone beat each of them, almost to death, with a baseball bat. Then they were shot in the head and left by the roadside.

Chicago's world of organised crime, but it did not stop him. Instead, it was the work of the Internal Revenue Service, who uncovered $200,000 worth of unpaid federal income tax, that finally led to his arrest on charges of income tax avoidance in 1931.

THE IMPACT OF GANGSTERS

EXTRACT B

From a history of the USA, published in 1997.

It is difficult to enforce a law which large numbers of people are prepared to break. Right from the start there were very large numbers of people – particularly in the cities – who were prepared to defy the prohibition law. American citizens got used to seeing people driving lorries laden with beer barrels in broad daylight through busy cities – with the police and prohibition agents apparently doing nothing to stop them.

Gangsters had existed before Prohibition, but the alcohol ban helped make them more successful. Their activities had a big effect on major US cities, because they:

- Were extremely violent: by November 1924, there had been around 200 gang-related murders in Chicago.
- Controlled local politicians: Chicago's mayor, Big Bill Thompson, was re-elected in 1927 because of support from gangsters.
- Turned ordinary citizens into criminals: residents of Chicago's South Side helped to illegally manufacture around 200 gallons of alcohol a day.

The work of gangsters also helped to make Prohibition ineffective. They bribed low paid prohibition agents, preventing them from enforcing the law. This proved highly effective and by 1929, alcohol consumption was back to around 70 per cent of its 1914 level and New York was home to over 32,000 speakeasies. These problems, combined with difficulties in enforcement and the work of campaign groups like the Association Against the Prohibition Amendment, eventually changed the policy of the national government. In 1933, the national ban on alcohol was ended.

EXAM-STYLE QUESTION

A03   **A04**

 SKILLS   CRITICAL THINKING, REASONING, DECISION MAKING, ADAPTIVE LEARNING, CREATIVITY, INNOVATION

Study Extract B.
Extract B suggests that large numbers of people were prepared to defy the prohibition law.
How far do you agree with this interpretation?
Use Extract B, Sources I and J and your own knowledge to explain your answer. **(16 marks)**

HINT

This question targets your ability to use source material and your own knowledge to evaluate a historical interpretation.

ACTIVITY

1 In pairs, write a 1 minute speech that argues either:
- Prohibition was a success or
- Prohibition was a failure.
2 Join up with another pair that has argued the opposite case. Perform your speeches to each other. Write down the key points the other pair makes.
3 Write a reply to the other pair's points, using evidence to challenge at least one of them. Read it out to the other pair.

RECAP

RECALL QUIZ

1 Name one piece of legislation passed in the 1920s to restrict immigration.
2 Which areas of Europe did the USA want to prevent emigration from?
3 How many strikes were there in 1919 in the USA: 1,200, 3,600 or 5,500?
4 Who was the attorney general who launched the raids on suspected communists and other radicals during the 'Red Scare'?
5 In what year were Sacco and Vanzetti accused of committing an armed robbery in Braintree, Massachusetts?
6 What was the name used to describe segregation laws?
7 Which race of people did the KKK believe were the best?
8 Which theory did John Scopes teach in Tennessee that led to his arrest?
9 Which famous partnership seized around 5 million bottles of illegal alcohol in the 1920s?
10 How much did Al Capone earn from organised crime each year: $1.5 million, $10.5 million or $105 million?

CHECKPOINT

STRENGTHEN

S1 What facts or ideas show that the US government did not want immigrants from southern and eastern Europe?
S2 Describe the ways black people were persecuted.
S3 In what ways did the values of fundamentalism and temperance affect US society in the 1920s?

CHALLENGE

C1 What links can you find between:
- attitudes towards immigration and the 'Red Scare'?
- attitudes towards black Americans and the KKK?
- the 'Monkey Trial' and Prohibition?

C2 Explain one of the links you have identified in C1.
C3 Find and explain a link between a topic in this chapter and one in Chapter 1.

How confident do you feel about your answers to these questions? If you're not sure you answered them well, try creating notes on how each event, policy or organisation listed in this chapter increased social tensions.

SUMMARY

- Many Americans preferred immigrants from northern and western Europe.
- A number of laws were introduced in the 1920s to restrict immigration.
- Some Americans feared communists and anarchists, which led to the Palmer Raids on suspected radicals in 1919 and 1920.
- Sacco and Vanzetti were tried (1921) and executed (1927) for murder, revealing anti-immigrant attitudes in the US legal system.
- Black Americans faced racist attitudes from some white Americans, resulting in segregation, violence and restrictions on their freedom.
- The KKK was a powerful organisation that persecuted black Americans.
- American Protestants were divided into fundamentalists and modernists.
- John Scopes was tried and fined for teaching Darwin's Theory of Evolution in 1925.
- Prohibition was introduced in 1919, which helped to improve the health of Americans.
- Gangsters resisted Prohibition and built up powerful organisations based around the sale and drinking of illegal alcohol.

EXAM GUIDANCE: PART (B) QUESTIONS

Study Sources A and B.

SOURCE A

From a speech by Senator Ellison Smith of South Carolina, given in April 1924 to the US Congress.

I think we now have enough people in our country for us to shut the door and to breed up a pure American citizenship. I would make this not a place of escape for the oppressed of all countries, but a country to develop that splendid type of man that has made America the best nation in her progress and in her power.

SOURCE B

From a speech by Congressman London, given to Congress in April 1921.

To prevent immigration means to cripple the United States. Our most developed industrial states are those which have had the largest immigration. Our most backward states industrially and educationally are those which had little immigration. By this Bill to restrict immigration we, who have escaped the horrors of the First World War, will refuse a place of safety to the victims of the war.

AO3

SKILLS ANALYSIS, ADAPTIVE LEARNING, CREATIVITY

Question to be answered: How far does Source A support the evidence of Source B about immigration to the USA in the 1920s? Explain your answer. (8 marks)

1 **Analysis Question 1: What is the question type testing?**
In this question, you have to demonstrate that you can comprehend, interpret and cross-refer sources. In this question, that means you can see similarity and difference between two sources in what they say about immigration to the USA.

2 **Analysis Question 2: What do I have to do to answer the question well?**
You have to write about points and areas of agreement and difference between the two sources that you are given. Do NOT be tempted to tell the examiner what each source says. The examiner will already know that! Go straight for the agreements and differences. You might, for example, say, 'The main areas of agreement between the two sources are ..', or 'The sources both agree that …' or 'The two sources differ about …'.

3 **Analysis Question 3: Are there any techniques I can use to make it very clear that I am doing what is needed to be successful?**
This is an 8-mark question, and you need to be sure you leave enough time to answer the (c) part, which is worth 16 marks. So you need to get straight in to your answer. Divide it into three parts. In the first paragraph, identify areas and points of agreement; in the second paragraph, identify differences. Remember to quote from the source material to support what you are saying. Your final paragraph should explain the extent of the support or agreement between the two sources. That means, how strongly they agree or disagree.

You must identify both agreement and difference. You will get up to 5 marks for doing this and for supporting what you have selected with material from the sources (but a maximum of 4 if you do 'just one side'). There are 3 additional marks for explaining the extent to which one source supports the other.

Answer

The sources agree that America is a place that people wanted to migrate to. Source A says that it is 'an escape for all the oppressed of all countries', suggesting that immigrants went to America to escape problems in their home country. Source B agrees, as it says America was 'a place of safety to the victims of the war'.

However, the two sources disagree on the impact of immigration. Source A suggests it was not good for America, saying 'I think we now have enough people in our country'. In contrast, Source B says 'to prevent immigration means to cripple the United States.' They also disagree on attitudes towards immigrants. The speaker in Source A dislikes them, suggesting they make America less 'pure', whereas Source B claims the most successful states have 'the largest immigration.'

To conclude, Source A only supports the evidence of Source B a small amount.

What are the strengths of this answer?
- *The agreements and differences between the sources are clearly identified in separate paragraphs.*
- *The points made in each paragraph are supported by appropriate quotations from the sources.*

What are the weaknesses of this answer?
- *The conclusion is weak, as the student does not explain the extent of support Source A offers Source B. A stronger answer would explain the measuring word used.*

Answer checklist
- ☐ Identifies similarities
- ☐ Identifies differences
- ☐ Provides information from the sources to support the statements
- ☐ Considers the extent of the support/disagreement. Which is stronger?

3. THE USA IN DEPRESSION, 1929–33

LEARNING OBJECTIVES

■ Understand the causes of the Wall Street Crash and its significance

■ Understand the impact of the Great Depression on the US economy and society

■ Understand the effectiveness of Hoover's measures to tackle the Great Depression.

During the 1920s, the stock market based at the New York Stock Exchange on Wall Street was very successful. However, in 1929 it suffered a crash as Americans began to sell their shares at whatever price they could get. As their desperation increased, prices decreased sharply. Nevertheless, they kept selling and around 1.5 million Americans, out of a population of 120 million, faced financial ruin. Their losses were just the beginning. Soon the entire economy had sunk into a period of low economic activity that became known as the Great Depression. From mid-1930 onwards, international trade, industrial production and farm prices all dropped, while unemployment, homelessness and bank closures rose to record levels.

In the desperate times that followed, Americans did what they had to for survival. Some travelled around the country, taking any job they could. Others expressed their anger towards the government, setting up a protest camp in the capital. Some homeless people settled into shanty towns, naming them after the man they blamed for their problems. That man, President Herbert Hoover, did what he could to find a solution, but the problems were too deep-rooted to be solved quickly. In the eyes of his citizens this was not good enough. He had failed to end the Depression, so they voted him out of his job.

3.1 CAUSES AND CONSEQUENCES OF THE WALL STREET CRASH (1929–30)

LEARNING OBJECTIVES

☐ Understand the causes of the Wall Street Crash and the consequences for investors and banks

☐ Understand the contribution the Wall Street Crash made to the Great Depression

☐ Understand other economic problems that led to the Great Depression.

CAUSES OF THE WALL STREET CRASH

During the 1920s, many Americans enjoyed 'playing the market' on Wall Street. It was a time when the value of shares continued to rise and it seemed easy to make money. In 1925, the combined value of the shares traded on Wall Street was around $34 billion, rising to $64 billion by 1929. However, things were not quite as good as they appeared. Ideally, the value of shares rises when a company is doing well, increasing sales and making more profit. Investors see the company as healthy and want to buy its shares, in order to share in the profits. However, the growth in share value on Wall Street in 1929 occurred because:

- so many people were buying and selling shares (see Chapter 1, pages 10–11), which increased demand and drove up prices
- Americans had great confidence in their economy, believing that prices would keep on rising, so they were prepared to keep on buying
- a **bull pool** encouraged inexperienced investors to **speculate**, artificially increasing prices.

As a result, the New York Stock Exchange on Wall Street relied more on the confidence of investors than it did on successful businesses. When this confidence was weakened, the whole system began to collapse.

The first sign of trouble occurred when news spread in mid-1929 that stock market leaders had begun to sell their shares because they expected prices to fall. They recognised that the stock market was not aligned with the realities of the US economy. For example, two of America's most important industries, car manufacturing and construction, were in decline. At the same time, the **Federal Reserve** had begun to make it more difficult to borrow money for speculation. Fearing worse was to come, the most experienced investors pulled out of the stock market. The crash began when more followed their example and panic replaced confidence. By late October, most investors were desperately trying to sell their shares and prices dropped further (see below) until in mid-November they were low enough to bring some buyers back into the market. By then, many investors were ruined.

KEY TERMS

bull pool a group of traders who set out to artificially increase the price of a share by buying and selling it to each other repeatedly over a short period, in order to sell that share to less experienced investors at a profit

speculate buying goods or shares on the expectation that their price will rise in the short term, with a view to selling them on to make a profit

Federal Reserve a system of central banking in the USA, with a range of functions, including lending money to member banks

September 1929 Average share prices on the New York Stock Exchange reach their peak

24 October 1929 Black Thursday Around 13 million shares are traded and prices fall rapidly

29 October 1929 Black Tuesday After a brief recovery, 16 million shares are traded, the highest number so far

Early October 1929 Around 4 million shares are traded each day and prices begin to fall

24 October 1929 (afternoon) A team of leading bankers buy up shares in around 20 companies and calm the situation

13 November 1929 Share prices hit their lowest point

▲ Timeline of the Wall Street Crash

▼ Share prices in 1928–29

COMPANY	3 MARCH 1928	3 SEPTEMBER 1929	13 NOVEMBER 1929
Woolworths	$1.81	$2.51	$0.52
Radio Corp.	$0.94	$5.05	$0.28
AT&T (telephone company)	$0.77	$3.04	$1.97
Westinghouse (electrical goods)	$0.92	$2.89	$1.02
General Motors (cars)	$1.40	$1.89	$0.36

CONSEQUENCES OF THE WALL STREET CRASH

The Wall Street Crash directly affected investors as share values continued to drop until mid-November 1929. By this point, shares had lost around $26 billion in value, which was a third of what they were worth in September. This was a big problem for investors who had bought on the margin (see Chapter 1, page 10), because brokers, who had suffered huge losses themselves, demanded immediate repayment of loans. Investors had to take money from their savings in order to pay back what they owed, which put considerable strain on banks. If the investor had no savings, they had to sell their possessions to raise money.

The problem banks now had to cope with was **liquidity**. Their customers demanded cash, but banks do not literally keep customers' money in the safe. Instead, they invest it in the stock market (and in 1929 made losses along with everyone else) and loan it to companies and other customers. So, when customers asked for their savings back in cash, banks had to ask companies and people with loans to repay them immediately so that they could return the money to their customers. With little spare money, banks stopped making loans to businesses. If these measures did not provide the bank with enough cash, they were forced to close down. Customers lost their savings and businesses lost an important source of credit.

KEY TERM

liquidity the amount an organisation holds in cash, or in a form that is easily turned into cash

EXTEND YOUR KNOWLEDGE

SUICIDES

It is a popular myth that the suicide rate increased rapidly after the crash, with hundreds of investors throwing themselves from high windows. In reality, the suicide rate rose only a little from 13.6 per 100,000 in 1928 to 15.7 in 1930. It is also a myth that most people who took their own lives jumped out of windows. Instead, failed investors jumped into rivers, breathed in gas or shot themselves.

A man trying to sell his car after the Wall Street Crash.

THE WALL STREET CRASH AND THE GREAT DEPRESSION

The crash was a major factor in bringing about the Great Depression in the USA, although it was not the only cause (see pages 53-56). Some Americans, including those who had invested in the stock market, or worked for a company that did so, lost their savings or had to cope with wage cuts. The result was a reduction in consumer spending, especially on luxury items like cars and electrical appliances, which meant newer industries struggled to find buyers for their products.

This created a difficult atmosphere for business, which was made worse by the problem of credit. Before the crash, companies could get a loan from their bank or sell shares on the stock market to raise money. This helped them to grow their business, or meet their day-to-day running costs. Afterwards, the supply of credit was cut off and businesses had to change their approach. They invested less, cut down their production and began to get rid of workers. With lower production rates, and fewer wage earners, the US economy began to struggle.

SOURCE B

From *Only Yesterday*, published in 1931 by an American academic. He is describing the economic problems in the 1920s.

When stock profits vanished during the Wall Street Crash and new instalment buyers became harder to find and men and women were wondering how they could afford the next payment on the car or the radio or the furniture, manufacturers were forced to operate their enlarged and all-too-productive factories on a reduced and unprofitable basis as they waited for buying power to recover.

SOURCE C

From a telegram, written in 1929 by an American business leader. He is describing the future after the Wall Street Crash.

The recent collapse of stock market prices has no significance to the real wealth of the American people as a whole. Paper profits and paper losses in stocks will not change people's total demand for either necessities or luxuries to any considerable extent. Future business prosperity will continue to rest, as it has in the past, on our industrial productivity and well-informed business leadership.

EXAM-STYLE QUESTION

A03

SKILLS ANALYSIS, ADAPTIVE LEARNING, CREATIVITY

Study Sources B and C.

How far does Source B support the evidence of Source C about the consequences of the Wall Street Crash? Explain your answer.   **(8 marks)**

HINT

This question targets your ability to comprehend, interpret and cross-refer sources, so make sure you quote from both sources in your answer.

ACTIVITY

1 In groups, create a scene for a class roleplay on the Wall Street Crash. Plan one of the following scenes:
- the New York Stock Exchange at its peak in September 1929
- Wall Street on 24 October 1929, including the attempt to calm the market
- Black Tuesday at the New York Stock Exchange, 29 October 1929
- customers at a bank in November 1929
- a family meeting to discuss the future in November 1929
- a board meeting to discuss a company's future in November 1929.

2 Take it in turns to perform the roleplays. Write down a summary of the message of each scene after you have watched it.

3 Use these summaries to write a short report on the Wall Street Crash, which includes causes, events and consequences.

OTHER CAUSES OF THE GREAT DEPRESSION

As well as the Wall Street Crash, other economic problems in the USA contributed to the Great Depression and prolonged its impact.

UNDER-CONSUMPTION

A central feature of the Depression was that Americans reduced their spending on consumer goods. This was because there was a limited market for things like new cars, radios and houses. Those who could afford it had bought them, but most could not because of the huge gap between the rich and poor, between farmers and workers in new industries, as well as between black and white people. This gap meant 71 per cent of Americans were on low incomes of below $2,500 a year and lacked the **purchasing power** to buy luxury consumer goods and new houses. Once the market was **saturated**, the well-paid workers who produced these goods began to lose their jobs, weakening their purchasing power too.

OVER-PRODUCTION IN INDUSTRY

The challenges facing the older industries, including coal, textiles and the railroads, have been outlined in Chapter 1 (see pages 22–23). In addition to this, by the late 1920s, the car and construction industries were also in decline. Before the crash, car sales had fallen by a third in 1929 and the amount spent on construction had dropped by $2 billion since 1926. All these industries were still producing goods to sell, but fewer people were buying them, which meant prices began to fall.

FALLING INCOME OF FARMERS

The 1920s was a difficult decade for the third of the population who worked in agriculture. Over-production and falling demand created huge problems for

KEY TERMS

purchasing power the amount of goods people are able to afford with their income

saturated when there are no more potential customers for a product or service in a market

farmers (see Chapter 1, pages 20–22). Key features of the Great Depression, like falling prices, lower incomes and rising unemployment already existed for them in the 1920s. As such, the beginning of the Great Depression did not signal a dramatic change for those in rural areas who were already struggling.

SOURCE D

A photo of a dust storm on the Great Plains in the 1930s. It shows the environmental problems farmers had to cope with.

However, the situation for farmers did grow even worse in the early 1930s, lowering economic activity still further. Between 1930 and 1931, there were severe droughts across the Great Plains of the USA. This area had already begun to suffer from soil erosion caused by intensive use of the land by farmers, but conditions were made far worse by the dust storms that began to strike in 1932. As a result, huge amounts of land became unusable, unemployment increased and incomes decreased. This was not a cause of the Great Depression, but it did make its impact greater.

FAILING BANKS

A strong economy relies on banks to protect people's savings, which can be used to buy goods and property, while providing loans to help businesses to grow. In the USA, banks had two major weaknesses:

- many banks had limited reserves of money available to them and no back-up if they needed help
- only a third of banks were part of the Federal Reserve System and each state had different banking regulations. This made it difficult for the government to help banks in a crisis.

These weaknesses made banks likely to be affected by a **'run'** and even before 1929, 5,172 US banks, around 20 per cent of the total, failed in the

KEY TERM

'run' when customers rush to take their money out of a bank because they have lost confidence in it

KEEPING THE BANK OPEN
Not all bankers facing a 'run' on their bank had to close their doors. Marriner Eccles, who ran a bank in Utah and went on to be chairman of the Federal Reserve, told his staff to work very slowly. With queues extending out the door, bank workers counted out withdrawals in low value bills at an agonisingly slow pace. This gave the bank longer to get people who owed them money to pay back their loans in order to meet customer demands. These desperate measures helped his bank to survive the 'run' because the bank had enough money to satisfy the customers making withdrawals.

1920s. Following the 1929 crash, customers saw banks failing and rushed to get their own savings out, in case their own bank failed. The 'run' that banks feared was happening.

Bank failures contributed to the Great Depression because banks took spending power away from consumers and cut off loans to businesses. The most significant failure occurred in December 1930, when the New York City Bank left 400,000 people without their savings. In the absence of a rescue attempt by the Federal Reserve, $286 million were lost by its customers. Faith in the banking system collapsed and many more banks, along with the businesses they supported, suffered the consequences.

PROBLEMS IN EUROPE

Not all of the problems that led to the Great Depression were American. One of the most important contributing factors was actually the First World War in Europe. During the war, the USA had lent the Allied nations huge sums of money, which needed to be repaid in the 1920s. Most European nations could not pay back these loans, so they used new loans from the USA to help pay off their First World War debts. This was a cycle that relied on a continuous flow of money from America, which could not continue forever, especially after the Great Depression had begun in the USA itself. Once the money supply was cut, the means to buy American goods in Europe was lost along with it and so American exports dropped, hitting company profits.

Another problem was that major European nations had begun to cut themselves off from America in the early 1930s. They did this in a number of ways:

- high tariffs were placed on American goods
- Germany tried to become **self-sufficient**
- Britain set up a trading agreement within its own empire.

These actions closed off another market for American goods, damaging international trade. This situation was influenced by a crisis in 1931 when several major European banks failed, resulting in huge withdrawals of cash. During one 6-week period, around $1,105 million were withdrawn in Europe. This led to bank failures and weakened international trade still further, the value of which had fallen from $36 billion in 1929 to around $12 billion 3 years later.

ACTIVITY

1 Make your own copy of Figure 3.1 on A3 paper, but leave out the arrows.
2 Draw an arrow from each cause to one feature of the Great Depression you think it could be linked to. For example, the Wall Street Crash to falling investment.
3 Explain, on the arrow, how the cause led to the feature of the Great Depression.

Few Americans could afford to buy luxury consumer goods.

The Wall Street Crash hit investors, banks and some businesses hard.

The Great Depression (1929–41)

Rising	**Falling**
Unemployment	Industrial production
Homelessness	Prices
Bank failures	International trade
Business closures	Investment

The banking system was badly organised and poorly run.

Industry and agriculture were struggling.

Europe cut itself off from the USA.

▲ **Figure 3.1** Causes of the Great Depression

3.2 THE IMPACT OF THE GREAT DEPRESSION

LEARNING OBJECTIVES

- ☐ Understand the impact of the Great Depression on banking, agriculture and industry
- ☐ Understand the effects of the Great Depression on people's lives, including unemployment and homelessness
- ☐ Understand the measures taken to help the poorest groups in US society to survive, including the construction of Hoovervilles and the Bonus March.

THE IMPACT ON BANKING

We have already seen how problems with banks were a cause of the Great Depression, but they were also victims of it. Once Americans lost confidence in the banks, they withdrew all their savings. A 'run' on the bank usually meant they had to close down because they could not get sufficient money quickly enough to repay customers. The result of this weakness was that out of the 25,000 banks the USA had in 1929, around 9,000 closed between 1930 and 1933. These banks held the savings of 9 million Americans, who lost about $2.5 billion due to their closure.

THE IMPACT ON AGRICULTURE

THE ECONOMIC CRISIS

In 1929 prices for agricultural goods, like wheat and cotton, were already low. Nevertheless, as a result of continued over-production at home and increased production abroad, prices continued to fall. At their lowest point, they reached 60 per cent below the 1929 level and farm incomes fell dramatically. Between them, American farmers earned around $6 billion in 1929, but by 1932 this had fallen to $2 billion. This made it almost impossible to continue to pay off **mortgages** and other debts which resulted in a third of American farmers losing their land.

In response to these economic problems, many farmers struggled to find ways to survive. This led to:

- Protest: farms that had been taken from their original owners due to debt were put up for auction. Sometimes the local community took action and forced the auctioneer to sell to them at a very low price, after which it was returned to its owner. Such actions, however, were rare.
- Migration: in the early 1930s, around 2 million people moved from rural to urban areas. However, the Depression turned cities into unpleasant places with large numbers of unemployed people and the rate of migration slowed considerably by the mid-1930s.

SOURCE E

From a newspaper report written in 1931 describing the effects of the drought in Arkansas.

The long drought that ruined hundreds of Arkansas farms last summer had a dramatic sequel late today when some 500 farmers, most of them white men and many of them armed, marched on the business section of this town shouting that they must have food for themselves and their families. They announced their intention to take it from the stores unless it were provided from some other source for free.

SOURCE F

From a statement given to the US government in 1932, describing conditions in rural America.

The roads of the West and the Southwest teem with hunger hitchhikers. The camp fires of the homeless are seen along every railroad track. I saw men, women and children walking over the hard roads. Most of them were tenant farmers who had lost their all in the recent slump in wheat and cotton.

KEY TERM

tenant farmer a farmer who rents land, rather than owns it

EXAM-STYLE QUESTION

AO3

SKILLS ANALYSIS, ADAPTIVE LEARNING, CREATIVITY

Study Sources E and F.
How far does Source E support the evidence of Source F about the impact of the Depression on agriculture?
Explain your answer   (8 marks)

HINT

Don't just repeat what the sources say; compare them.

THE ENVIRONMENTAL CRISIS

Until the early 1930s, most farmers still had one further option available to them. They could work harder, grow more crops and rear more farm animals. Even though prices were falling, increased production would help maintain their income. However, this option was taken away from them by an environmental crisis that caused a major problem for the states spread across an area that became known as the dustbowl (see Figure 3.2).

A drought, affecting 17 million Americans in the eastern USA, ruined crops in the summer of 1930. Then, with so much dry land, high winds created dust storms across the **Great Plains** in 1932. In April 1933, 179 small dust storms were recorded, of which 38 were severe **black blizzards**. These storms blew away the surface layer where plants grew, leaving the land too poor for farming. Left with little land to grow or raise livestock on, farms failed, leaving the farmer, his family and his workers without any source of income.

In such hopeless circumstances, many Americans from Oklahoma, Arkansas and other states on the Great Plains, chose to migrate west. Between 1930 and 1935, around a million people left their farms on the Great Plains and headed to states where they thought work was available. A popular destination was California, where migrant labourers, nicknamed **Okies**, were required to pick fruit and harvest crops for starvation wages. Sheltering in tents or hastily constructed cabins, Okies lived through some of the worst conditions that Americans experienced during the Great Depression.

KEY TERMS

Great Plains an area of grassland over 1.3 million square km in size, covering much of central North America

black blizzard a powerful dust storm, lifting dark-coloured bits of soil up to 2.5 km into the air and rolling across the landscape

Okies the name given to migrants from the Great Plains, including Oklahoma, who travelled westwards in search of work

---

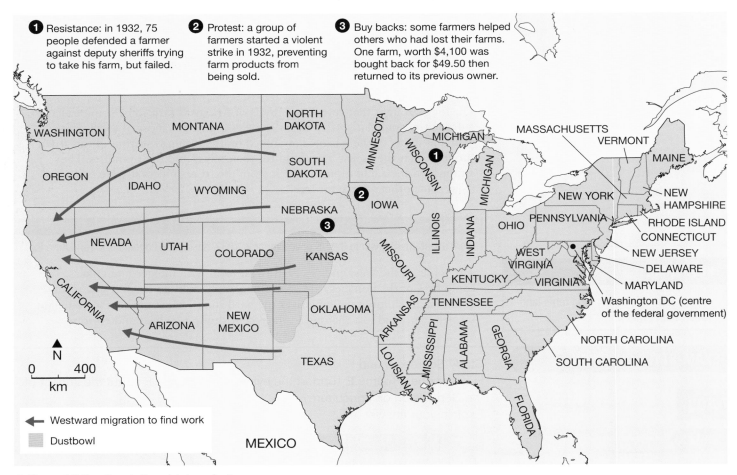

1 Resistance: in 1932, 75 people defended a farmer against deputy sheriffs trying to take his farm, but failed.

2 Protest: a group of farmers started a violent strike in 1932, preventing farm products from being sold.

3 Buy backs: some farmers helped others who had lost their farms. One farm, worth $4,100 was bought back for $49.50 then returned to its previous owner.

Westward migration to find work

Dustbowl

▲ **Figure 3.2** Reactions to the crisis in agriculture

THE IMPACT ON INDUSTRY

The biggest problem for American industry was the fall in demand for goods. Other countries did not want, or could not afford, US goods, which meant the physical amount the USA exported decreased by 39 per cent between 1929 and 1932. Demand was a particular problem for industries that produced luxury goods as customers from around the world, as well as in the USA itself, no longer had the spare cash to buy them. For example, car manufacturers sold 3.5 million fewer cars in 1933 than they had in 1929. This meant newer industries had to face the same difficulties that had affected older ones during the 1920s (see pages 22–23).

Reductions in demand also led to companies cutting prices to try to sell goods. This turned national business profits of $9,628 million in 1929 into losses of $3,017 million in 1932. In an attempt to cope with these problems, industries:

- Cut wages: in manufacturing wages fell by almost 50 per cent between 1929 and 1933.
- Reduced production and working hours: US steel workers had their hours cut as production in steel mills dropped 38 per cent in the first year of the Depression.
- Got rid of workers: Ford made half of his workforce in Detroit redundant.

If these solutions did not result in profits, factories closed down. By 1933, around 70,000 factories had been forced to take this option and many Americans suffered as a result.

Demand for goods drops

Company profits fall

Workers laid off

Less money to buy goods

Demand for goods drops

▲ **Figure 3.3** The negative cycle of economic depression

THE IMPACT ON PEOPLE'S LIVES

UNEMPLOYMENT IN THE 1930S

During the Great Depression, millions of Americans lost their jobs. In 1929, 3.2 per cent of the potential workforce was unemployed, but this had risen to 24.9 per cent by 1933. In certain regions, where people worked in steelmaking or car manufacturing, the situation could be even worse. In these areas, unemployment reached as high as 50 per cent. However, it was not just the unemployed who faced difficulties. For the rest of the workforce who remained in their jobs, underemployment was a serious problem. Up to one-third of people had to work part-time, which meant even those with jobs had to cope with lower incomes.

EFFECTS OF UNEMPLOYMENT

The immediate effect of unemployment on a family was a decline in their living standards. Utilities like electricity were cut off and household spending on fuel and food was reduced. As a result, people's health suffered. For example, in 1932, 20,000 children in New York City did not have enough food. One magazine even claimed a sixth of the nation would die over the winter. This claim, although exaggerated, shows how bad Americans believed the situation had become by 1932.

By this time, some American families were struggling to fund themselves and had to rely on **relief**. Despite this need, there was not much support available, as there were no national benefits or help for the unemployed. Instead, they turned to their extended family, soup kitchens funded by private charities, or their local government. These groups could provide a little for them, but they did not have the funding to make a big difference.

KEY TERM

relief help from the local or state government for the poor, or other groups in need, which was either provided in the home, or in government institutions like poorhouses

KEY TERM

replacement rate the birth rate required to keep the population level the same without the influence of immigration

EXTEND YOUR KNOWLEDGE

US WORKERS IN THE SOVIET UNION
In 1930, the Soviet Union removed some restrictions on immigration because they wanted skilled foreign workers for their heavy industries. By 1932, around 10,000 Americans were working there. It was a decision they came to regret. As Soviet policy became harsher in the late 1930s many workers were sent to prison camps or shot.

EXTEND YOUR KNOWLEDGE

THE RESPONSE OF BLACK PEOPLE
Black people did take action to challenge their mistreatment. The National Association for the Advancement of Colored People (NAACP) made legal challenges against segregation. At the same time, black campaigners, like W.E.B. Du Bois and Marcus Garvey, worked hard to help improve the situation of black people.

A lack of relief had national consequences in the 1930s, including homelessness and protests, as well as significant social effects:

■ the average couple married 2 years later than they did in the 1920s
■ the birth rate fell below the **replacement rate**
■ between 1929 and 1931, the suicide rate increased by 14 per cent.

In such circumstances, many chose to leave their homes. Some people travelled across the USA searching for work (see page 62), while around 100,000 others applied for jobs in the Soviet Union.

EFFECTS ON DISADVANTAGED GROUPS

Some groups suffered more than others during the Great Depression. The table below shows how black people, immigrant workers, women and the elderly were affected by rising unemployment levels.

▼ The effect of the Great Depression on disadvantaged social groups

▼ GROUP	▼ EFFECT OF THE GREAT DEPRESSION
Black people	More likely to lose their job: half of black women in the workforce lost their jobs during the Depression. Faced racist threats: 40,000 people joined the Black Shirts, based in Atlanta, to campaign against black people in work.
Immigrant workers	Lost their jobs to white people: Mexican Americans, working in California and the Southwest, were replaced with white workers. Left or were deported: approximately 500,000 workers returned to Mexico in the early 1930s.
Women	Lost their jobs: household help was no longer affordable and around 25 per cent of women lost their jobs in domestic service. Some benefits: as a result of lower family incomes, around 25 per cent more women were able to find work outside the family home by the end of the Depression.
Elderly	Couldn't retire: many Americans had to work into their old age, as they could not afford to retire. Few benefits: only 11 states had pension schemes and just 15 per cent of industrial workers had a private plan. Most people had to rely on family for help in their old age.

HOMELESSNESS

Americans who could not pay their rent or keep up with their mortgage payments often lost their homes. In these circumstances, many relied on charities or local government to help them. For example, in 1931, New York City's government had to try and find accommodation for 20,000 children whose parents could no longer provide a home for them. However, with limited funding, local governments and private charities could not cope. This forced many homeless Americans to search for their own solutions.

SOURCE G

A photo of a migrant mother taken in the 1930s, taken by Dorothea Lange, a famous documentary photographer.

EXTEND YOUR KNOWLEGE

HARLEM RENT PARTIES

Self-help was a popular way to prevent homelessness. One method was a rent party, usually held by black Americans living in cities a few days before the rent was due. They sent round adverts, charging guests 25 cents for entry and more for drinks. Black jazz musicians would play music, earning themselves some money, while the hosts served up such things as pickled pig bladders, deep-fried pig intestines and illegal homemade beer and gin to their guests.

A popular option was to move from one place to another in search of work. Over a million men, as well as some women and family groups, travelled around by foot, car or railroad. This placed a huge strain on popular destinations. In California, even before the dust storms began, there were around 100,000 homeless people in 1931 looking for work. The state and local government, which was struggling to support its own residents, could not provide relief. Under these circumstances, the migrants, often referred to as hobos, kept on moving to find any temporary work they could.

HOOVERVILLES

The hobo lifestyle did not suit everyone and, if it was possible, the homeless tried to stay in or near their home towns. Often, they joined together to create a shanty town on empty land, building their accommodation from scrap materials. When joined by others, their population grew into the hundreds. In the biggest shanty towns, in New York City, Washington DC and St Louis, thousands could be found living without running water, basic facilities or permanent shelter. The residents called their towns 'Hoovervilles', because they blamed their problems on President Herbert Hoover.

A typical example of a Hooverville was the one built in Seattle. Here a man called Jesse Jackson declared himself mayor, took control of nine acres of land and encouraged others to join him. At first his settlement struggled. The city government did not approve and burnt down the settlement. However, the city's politicians quickly realised there was nowhere else for the homeless to go and officially acknowledged the Hooverville in 1932. As a result, men from various racial backgrounds lived there without an income, or the company of women and children. They led a difficult life, helped only by small donations from charities and the hope of getting a job and moving back into the city.

THE BONUS MARCHERS

Congress had passed a law in 1924 giving First World War veterans a bonus of up to $625 each to make up for the wages they lost while fighting for their country. There was only one catch. Most would have to wait until 1945 to receive their bonus. During the boom years of the 1920s, this was acceptable, but when the hard times of the Great Depression struck, the veterans felt they needed the money straight away. To get the government to listen to their demands, 20,000 people, known as the Bonus Marchers, marched to Washington DC in 1932. They camped across the river from the **Capitol** while they waited for the US Congress to decide whether they would get their bonus.

President Herbert Hoover was against the idea because he was trying to gather support and funds for other methods to tackle the Depression (see pages 64–67). After fierce debate, Congress rejected the bonus bill on 17 June 1932, but made $100,000 available to help the Bonus Marchers pay for their journey home. Many took up Congress's offer, but up to 5,000 veterans stayed behind to maintain pressure on the government. Both sides now waited for the other to back down.

KEY TERM

Capitol a government building in which the US Congress meets

SOURCE H

The Bonus Marcher's settlement in 1932. It has all the features of a typical Hooverville, including the tents the marchers lived in and the cars used to travel around and try to find work.

In this tense situation, Hoover was the first to act. He set a deadline for when all veterans should have left their camp. When this deadline passed, he asked the police to act. On 28 July 1932, the police tried to empty some buildings occupied by the marchers, but were attacked with rubbish and rubble. They withdrew and tried again, but this time shots were fired and two veterans were killed. The police were not prepared for this and pulled out.

Later that day, Hoover sent in the US Army. Under the command of General Douglas MacArthur, infantry, cavalry, machine guns and tanks were all used to clear the camp. It was a powerful force and the veterans fled, chased by troops who burnt tents and **teargassed** marchers as they went. At the end of the day, the Bonus Marchers had been defeated, with 100 of them injured and one of their children killed. Nevertheless, they had achieved one victory. Hoover's reputation was destroyed.

EXAM-STYLE QUESTION

A01

Describe **two** key features of the Bonus Marchers.   **(6 marks)**

HINT

This question targets your ability to demonstrate knowledge and understanding of the key features of the period you have studied.

ACTIVITY

1 In pairs, create eight cards with a title on one side and a fact on the other side. Use these titles: 'Impact on banking', 'Impact on agriculture', 'Impact on industry', 'Impact on unemployment', 'Impact on disadvantaged groups', 'Impact on homelessness', 'Hoovervilles', 'Bonus Marchers'.

2 With a partner, place the cards fact side down then take it in turns to guess the fact on the other side of the card. If you are right, keep the card. If not, return it to the desk. The winner is the player who guesses the greatest number of cards.

3 Create a Venn diagram with three titles: 'Effects on the poorest', 'Effects on the middle classes', 'Effects on politicians'. Sort the cards into your diagram.

4 Write an explanation of who you think the Depression had the greatest impact on.

3.3 HOOVER'S REACTION TO THE GREAT DEPRESSION: INTERVENTION AND VOLUNTEERISM

LEARNING OBJECTIVES

■ Understand the beliefs that affected Hoover's actions during the Great Depression

■ Understand the measures that Hoover took to tackle the Great Depression, including intervention in the economy and promoting volunteerism

■ Understand the impact of Hoover's actions on different groups.

HOOVER'S BELIEFS

During and after the Great Depression, the Republican president, Herbert Hoover, was heavily criticised. Many Americans believed he had not done enough to help them, accusing him of not taking enough action. However, the real picture is more complex. Hoover worked hard to fight the Depression, but his political beliefs limited how much action he would allow the government to take. These were:

■ Volunteerism: Hoover thought that the federal government did not have the right to force people to do things. That would be an infringement of their personal liberties. He saw the federal government's role as bringing together the state and local governments, as well as businessmen, to encourage them to act in a way which would help the economy. So he encouraged business leaders not to cut jobs or wages; he did not demand that they did this.

■ Self-reliance: individuals should be able to look after themselves and not become dependent on government or charity to survive.

Hoover's views were not unusual and reflected the beliefs of those people who supported the Republican Party. They believed it was not the job of the government to tell the business world how to operate or tell people how to live their lives. This belief in **laissez-faire** had helped make America rich in the 1920s and if left alone business would restore wealth. Hoover held these beliefs too, but he knew that the crisis was so great that action was needed.

KEY TERM

laissez-faire (*French: let people do as they choose*) the belief that government should not interfere in a country's economy and businesses and market forces should be left to fix any problems

HOOVER'S ACTIONS

Hoover used a range of methods to help banks, farms and industries, as well as tackle the problem of unemployment.

▼ Hoover's actions to end the Great Depression

▼ PROBLEM	▼ ACTIONS	▼ LIMITATIONS
Banks	Set up the **National Credit Corporation** (1931): $500 million was raised by businesses to help failing banks.	The NCC's investors were afraid to lose their money and spent very little of it.
	Established the **Reconstruction Finance Corporation** (1932): $2 billion was provided by the government to rescue banks and other key organisations.	The RFC was criticised for using government money to help banks rather than people.
Farms	**Agricultural Marketing Act** (1929): set up the Federal Farm Board to buy up crops from farmers.	The Farm Board built up huge amounts of extra goods and could not stop the fall in prices.
	Hawley-Smoot Tariff (1930): raised import duties on foreign food by 40 per cent to force Americans to buy their own goods.	Higher tariffs led other nations to do the same, reducing international trade.
	Federal Farm Loan Act (amended 1932): $125 million given to the Federal Land Banks to provide farm mortgages.	The Federal Land Banks provided mortgages, but did not help farmers repay them.
Industries	**National Business Survey Conference** (1929): Hoover arranged a meeting of 400 business executives. They made promises about production, expansion and wages.	Promises made in 1929 by major employers were broken as the Depression worsened.
	Moratorium on First World War debts (1931): USA would stop collecting debts for 18 months to give Europe time to recover.	The moratorium did not help enough to prevent the collapse of the international economy.
	Reconstruction Finance Corporation (1932): made money available for banks to loan to industries.	Most of the money loaned by the RFC went to the largest banks and companies.
Unemployment	**President's Emergency Committee for Employment** (1930–31): organised and encouraged donations for relief. It was later replaced by the **President's Organisation for Unemployment Relief**.	ECE and POUR could not raise the enormous sums of money needed to help the large numbers of unemployed.
	Public works: the government doubled its spending on federal government projects over 3 years. These projects, like the Grand Coulee Dam (Washington), created jobs for the unemployed.	Federal spending on public works was very low. It was $210 million in 1930, whereas states spent around $2 billion a year.
	Reconstruction Finance Corporation (1932): allowed the federal government to loan $300 million to states for relief.	States had to meet tough requirements in order to borrow the money. Only $30 million had been loaned by the end of 1932.

KEY TERM

moratorium a period during which debts do not have to be repaid (but are not cancelled), which provides time for debtors to gather funds

SOURCE I

From a speech by President Hoover to Congress, January 1932.

Our people through voluntary measures and through state and local actions are providing for distress. Through the organised action of employers they are making jobs available and easing the hardships of the depression. Through the work of national credit associations they are aiding the country greatly. The government's duty is to support these steps to make their efforts more effective.

► **Figure 3.4** Positive and negative effects of Hoover's measures

Hoover's measures did make a difference to the Great Depression. He took the first steps towards recovery, and Figure 3.4 illustrates the difference Hoover made to a range of groups. However, it also shows the problems those groups continued to face. The reality was that a huge economic crisis could not be solved overnight and needed more government support and **intervention** than the USA had ever seen before. No Republican president could ever take such radical action. It was no surprise when in 1932 the country voted in a Democrat president, Franklin Delano Roosevelt, who promised them 'a New Deal'.

KEY TERM

intervention action taken to change a situation

SOURCE J

From a report by the city manager of Cincinnati to Congress, given at the end of 1931.

Relief is given to a family one week and then they are pushed off for a week in the hope that somehow or other the breadwinner may find some kind of work. That, of course, is a very difficult problem because we are continually having evictions, and social workers are hard-put to find places for people whose furniture has been put out on the street.

EXTRACT A

From a book on modern world history, published in 1985.

The man who was President of the United States when the great depression began was Herbert Hoover. His answer to the problem was to do little or nothing. There had been other, though less serious depressions in the past and the country had recovered without any help from the government. Hoover thought the same thing would happen again. 'Prosperity', he said, 'is just around the corner.'

ACTIVITY

1 Study Extract A. How far do you agree with the author? Explain your answer.
2 In pairs, use Figure 3.4 to prepare for an interview with Hoover. Split up the roles.
   ■ In the role of interviewer, one person should prepare questions to challenge Hoover's actions.
   ■ In the role of Hoover, one person should make some notes to help defend Hoover's actions.
3 Conduct the interview, then create a successes and failures table to sum up the impact of Hoover's measures.

RECAP

RECALL QUIZ

1 Name the group of traders that encouraged inexperienced investors to speculate.
2 In what month and year did the Wall Street Crash occur?
3 How much value was lost on shares traded on the US stock exchange between September and November, 1929: $26 million, $26 billion or $260 billion?
4 Which two major industries were in decline during the late 1920s?
5 In what year did drought begin to cause problems for farmers on the Great Plains?
6 How many factories had closed down by 1933: 70,000, 100,000, 1 million?
7 Which racist group, based in Atlanta, campaigned against black people in work?
8 What was the name given to shanty towns established during the Great Depression?
9 In which city did the Bonus Marchers set up their protest camp?
10 Which act set up the Federal Farm Board in 1929?

CHECKPOINT

STRENGTHEN
S1 List and describe three causes of the Great Depression, including the Wall Street Crash.
S2 Select and summarise the main effects of the Great Depression.
S3 What facts or ideas show that Hoover intervened to end the Great Depression?

CHALLENGE
C1 What are your views on:
■ the significance of the Wall Street Crash as a cause of the Great Depression?
■ the most serious impact of the Great Depression?
■ the effectiveness of President Hoover?
C2 Find two pieces of evidence to support each of your views.
C3 Based on what you know, how would you explain why the Great Depression did not end in 1933.

How confident do you feel about your answers to these questions? If you're not sure you answered them well, try creating your own version of Figure 3.4. In the first thought bubble, write why people faced difficulties and in the second, write the main problem they experienced.

SUMMARY

■ Investors lost confidence in the stock market, causing the New York Stock Exchange to crash in October 1929.
■ The Wall Street Crash caused some banks to close and contributed to the Great Depression.
■ Under-consumption, over-production, problems in Europe and a weak central banking system all contributed towards the Depression.
■ Many farmers lost their land during the Depression and were forced to migrate in search of work.
■ Factory workers lost their jobs or had their wages and hours cut during the Depression.
■ Unemployment led to poverty, which affected black people, migrant workers, women and the elderly the most.
■ Homeless people took shelter in shanty towns known as 'Hoovervilles'.
■ First World War veterans marched to Washington DC in 1932, demanding the bonus that had been promised to them, but President Hoover sent in the army to force them to return home.
■ Hoover based his solutions to the Depression on his beliefs in associationalism, volunteerism and self-reliance.
■ Hoover introduced a range of measures to help banks, farms, industries and the unemployed.

EXAM GUIDANCE: PART (C) QUESTIONS

Study Extract C.

EXTRACT C

From a history of the USA, published in 1997.

The overall effect of the Wall Street Crash was to destroy the confidence in the country which had enabled the 1920s boom to take place. People who had money decided to keep it, rather than to invest it or buy goods. Those banks which survived the crash stopped making loans so the capital needed to keep industry going dried up. Companies decided to cut production, lay off workers and reduce wages. The good times were gone and the Great Depression was just beginning.

SOURCE A

From *Only Yesterday*, published in 1931 by an American academic. He is describing the economic problems in the 1920s.

When stock profits vanished during the Wall Street Crash and new instalment buyers became harder to find and men and women were wondering how they could afford the next payment on the car or the radio or the furniture, manufacturers were forced to operate their enlarged and all-too-productive factories on a reduced and unprofitable basis as they waited for buying power to recover.

SOURCE B

From a telegram, written in 1929 by an American business leader. He is describing the future after the Wall Street Crash.

The recent collapse of stock market prices has no significance to the real wealth of the American people as a whole. Paper profits and paper losses in stocks will not change people's total demand for either necessities or luxuries to any considerable extent. Future business prosperity will continue to rest, as it has in the past, on our industrial productivity and well-informed business leadership.

A03   **A04**

SKILLS CRITICAL THINKING, REASONING, DECISION MAKING, ADAPTIVE LEARNING, CREATIVITY, INNOVATION

Question to be answered: Extract C suggests that the Wall Street Crash destroyed the overall confidence in the country.

How far do you agree with this interpretation?

Use Extract C, Sources A and B and your own knowledge to explain your answer. (16 marks)

Analysis Question: What do I have to do to answer this question well?

■ You have to demonstrate that you can use two sources and your own knowledge in order to show how far you agree with a historian's interpretation of an event.

■ This is a 16-mark question and you must make sure you write a quick plan before you start. This is because it is important to organise your ideas and your own knowledge.

■ Do not be tempted to write all you know about the topic, but select those parts of your own knowledge that are directly relevant to the interpretation given in the question.

Your answer could look like this.

Paragraph 1: show how the first source supports and disagrees with the interpretation, and use your own knowledge to support this evaluation.

Paragraph 2: show how the second source supports and disagrees with the interpretation and use your own knowledge to support this evaluation.

Paragraph 3: reach an overall judgement that is supported by brief references to the most important points you have made in paragraphs 1 and 2.

Answer

Source A supports the view that confidence was destroyed. It says that stock profits were gone and production was cut. We know that the stock markets prices fell, losing $26 billion in value between September and November 1929. Production was also cut, as companies like US Steel reduced how much their factories were used.

Source B says something different. It claims that the stock market crash was insignificant and that the boom would continue. This is partly true because only 1.5 million Americans out of population of 120 million had invested in the stock market. Their losses could not explain why everyone's confidence was destroyed.

However Extract C does provide extra information to explain why confidence fell. It says that banks struggled, which is true because big banks like the New York City Bank failed in December 1930. This reduced investment in companies, who had to make savings. For example, wages in manufacturing fell by 50 per cent between 1929 and 1933. So a problem affecting some people also affected big businesses and confidence in the economy fell.

What are the strengths of this answer?
- *A sound understanding is shown of the two sources.*
- *The two sources are clearly linked to different areas of the interpretation, and agreements and disagreements are identified.*
- *Relevant contextual knowledge is used in support of the points made.*
- *The interpretation is challenged by the use of contextual knowledge where it goes beyond the information contained in the sources.*

What are the weaknesses of this answer?
- *The answer looks at the arguments for and against the interpretation using the two sources, own knowledge and the extract itself, but it does not answer the question 'how far?'.*
- *To get the very highest marks, the answer has to do more than say 'yes and no'. It has to consider the strength of the argument on each side. For example, it would be impressive to say that the extract and sources both indicate there were other reasons for the collapse in confidence, such as over-production.*

Answer checklist
- [ ] Identifies agreement and disagreement with the hypothesis
- [ ] Uses information from the two sources, the extract and own contextual knowledge
- [ ] Addresses 'how far?' by 'weighing' the evidence to see which side is most strongly supported.

4. ROOSEVELT AND THE NEW DEAL, 1933–41

LEARNING OBJECTIVES

☐ Understand the aims and significance of Roosevelt's actions during the early days of his presidency

☐ Understand the key features of the second New Deal and its impact

☐ Understand the long-term significance of second New Deal legislation.

In 1933, the Great Depression was far from over. By this time, the immediate crisis was in banking, as customers desperately withdrew their savings and bank after bank closed down. At the same time, long-term problems worsened: farm prices rapidly decreased, industries failed and the poor suffered. Made landless or unemployed, and with little support from the government, the poor were losing their homes and starving. The state governments, private charities and leading businessmen were running out of funds and ideas on what to do to make a difference.

Nevertheless, a new president, Franklin D. Roosevelt, was prepared to try a vast range of solutions. His proposals, known as the New Deal, involved strengthening the control of the federal government, giving the president the power to make real changes. In the short term, Roosevelt used farm subsidies, industrial codes and work relief programmes to help poor citizens. Once they had begun to improve things, he turned to long-term reforms. He gave the USA its first ever social security programme, improved the rights of workers, centralised control of the banks and electrified the nation's farms.

4.1 ROOSEVELT'S AIMS

LEARNING OBJECTIVES

▪ Understand the reasons why Roosevelt was elected president

▪ Understand the aims of the New Deal

▪ Understand the methods Roosevelt planned to use to put the New Deal into practice.

ELECTION OF 1932

In 1932, Americans had a tough choice. Stick with Hoover, giving his methods time to work, or risk change and give someone else a go. Their alternative, Franklin D. Roosevelt, sometimes known as FDR, tried to make the choice an easy one. He promised voters that, like Hoover, he believed in a balanced budget. However, he also offered them something new. Unlike the previous president, Roosevelt said he would use federal government money to help the unemployed directly.

EXTEND YOUR KNOWLEDGE

FRANKLIN D. ROOSEVELT
Roosevelt had contracted polio in 1921 when he was 39 years old. The polio paralysed Roosevelt from the waist down, though he later managed to stand and walk very short distances with the help of leg braces. Despite his disability, he was elected governor of New York in 1929. When he was elected president in 1932, the White House had to have ramps fitted for Roosevelt's wheelchair. Despite this, many people did not know of his disability. He was usually photographed from a distance when standing and pictures of him in a wheelchair were not made public.

SOURCE A

From a radio broadcast by President Hoover, February 1931.

The Federal Government has taken on many new responsibilities in the last few decades, and will probably assume more in the future. But there is an essential principle that should be maintained in these matters. I am convinced that where Federal action is essential, then in most cases it should limit its responsibilities to helping the states and local communities, and that it should not replace the role of states or local government.

During the election campaign, Roosevelt called his plans 'a new deal for the American people' and 23 million voters agreed to give them a try. His willingness to take action ensured that 42 out of the 48 states voted for him. They also gave his party, the Democrats, a majority in Congress. As a result, in March 1933, he took office as president with a Congress who would authorise his decisions. On his inauguration day, he promised to get Americans back to work, help them keep their homes and protect their savings.

SOURCE B

From Roosevelt's Inaugural Address to Congress, March 1933.

Our greatest primary task is to put people to work. This is no unsolvable problem if we face it wisely and courageously. It can be accomplished in part by direct recruiting by the government itself, treating the task just like we would treat an emergency of a war. However, at the same time, through this employment, we can accomplish greatly needed projects to stimulate and reorganize the use of our country's natural resources.

EXAM-STYLE QUESTION

A03

SKILLS ANALYSIS, ADAPTIVE LEARNING, CREATIVITY

Study Sources A and B.
How far does Source A support the evidence of Source B about the role of the government in ending the Great Depression? Explain your answer.   **(8 marks)**

HINT

This question targets your ability to comprehend, interpret and cross-refer sources.

AIMS OF THE NEW DEAL

Roosevelt had three main aims, outlined in the table below, which his New Deal set out to achieve.

▽ AIM	▽ DESIRED OUTCOME
Recovery	An increased income for farmers and farm workers. Higher rates of industrial production. An end to the banking crisis.
Relief	States provided with enough money to meet the immediate needs for relief from hunger and poverty. Short-term work relief projects are available for the unemployed.
Reform	A social security system that looks after US citizens. Improvements in the way banks and businesses were run to secure long-term recovery.

His aims were ambitious, especially in a country where people had little daily contact with the federal government. To achieve them, he tried to:
- gain support, using radio broadcasts called 'fireside chats' to share his message directly with the American people
- utilise his majority in Congress to turn New Deal policies into law
- restore economic activity by using government money voted for by Congress to create jobs. This was known as '**priming the pump**' (see Figure 4.1)
- expand the federal government by setting up several new agencies to organise recovery and handle relief.

KEY TERM

priming the pump government spending to create jobs, meaning workers have more money to buy goods, which in turn increases demand for goods and creates more jobs

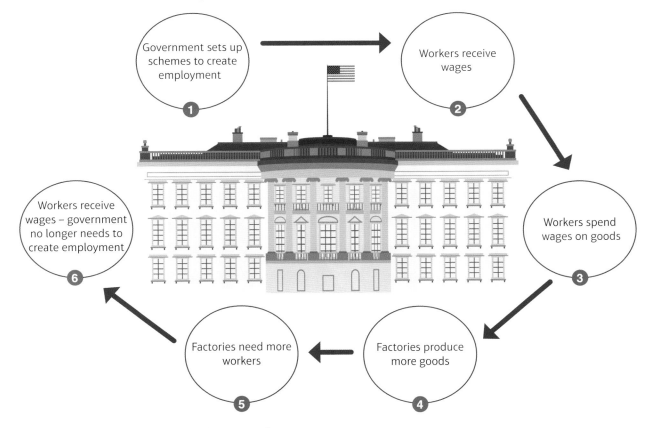

▲ **Figure 4.1** Roosevelt's belief in 'priming the pump'

ACTIVITY

1 Look back at Hoover's policies on page 65. Then create a table with three columns, using each of Roosevelt's aims (on page 73) as the headings. Add examples from Hoover's presidency that fit these aims.
2 Study Source A, Source B and Figure 4.1. Identify the most significant difference between Hoover's approach to the Depression and Roosevelt's.
3 Explain why, in no more than 100 words, Roosevelt's approach appealed to voters.

4.2 THE FIRST HUNDRED DAYS AND THE ALPHABET AGENCIES

LEARNING OBJECTIVES

☐ Understand the key features of the First Hundred Days

☐ Understand the role of the Alphabet Agencies in tackling the Depression

☐ Understand the policies followed to help farmers, factory workers and the unemployed.

THE FIRST HUNDRED DAYS

KEY TERM

Brains Trust a group of government officials, including experts in economics, government and law, who advised Roosevelt on New Deal policies

Roosevelt started work straight away, using his first 100 days in office to introduce a number of measures to tackle the Depression. He took advice from a group called the **Brains Trust** and once he had a plan in mind, he requested that Congress pass the laws required to put it into practice. Congress met for a special emergency session from 9 March to 16 June 1933 and helped Roosevelt set up relief programmes and establish new agencies to organise them.

SOURCE C

A photograph of Roosevelt giving a 'fireside chat' over the radio.

To help ensure these plans were a success, Roosevelt used modern technology to get the nation's support. On 30 separate occasions, he talked to ordinary Americans over the radio. In these 'fireside chats' the president explained new laws and agencies, using plain English and an informal tone. It was the first time a president had done this and it was very popular, encouraging ordinary Americans to feel he was on their side.

ACHIEVEMENTS OF THE FIRST HUNDRED DAYS

TACKLING THE BANKING CRISIS

The first challenge the new president had to deal with was the financial crisis. The banking system was in difficulty, as Hoover had not been able to stop huge numbers of banks from closing down. Roosevelt needed time to sort out the banks, so he asked Congress to pass the Emergency Banking Act, which closed all banks for 4 days. Federal checks were carried out and only 'financially sound' banks were allowed to reopen. To further restore confidence, Roosevelt talked about the banks in his first fireside chat on 12 March 1933, asking Americans to deposit their savings once again.

Roosevelt's banking strategy worked and by the end of March, Americans had deposited $1 million in their banks. This was a turning point because before Roosevelt's measures people had been rushing to take their savings out. The immediate crisis was over and Roosevelt took further steps to save the banks, passing a law to **insure** bank deposits of up to $2,500 and restricting how banks could use the money. People knew that even if a bank failed they would get up to $2,500 back. These measures restored confidence in the US financial system and the aim of recovery was partly achieved.

NEW LAWS AND THE ALPHABET AGENCIES

With the immediate financial crisis under control, Roosevelt turned to the other economic problems. With his support, Congress passed laws to:

- Solve the problems in agriculture: the Agricultural Adjustment Act set up the Agricultural Adjustment Administration (AAA) to help farmers.
- Tackle the problems in industry: the National Industrial Recovery Act (NIRA) established the National Recovery Administration (NRA), which wrote rules for industries to follow.
- Help the unemployed: Federal Emergency Relief Administration (FERA) provided relief payments.
- Save money: the Economy Act reduced government running costs by 25 per cent, which lowered federal spending by around $450 million.
- Raise funds: the Beer and Wine Revenue Act was the first step towards the end of Prohibition, making it legal to buy and sell alcohol below 3.2 per cent, which the government taxed, raising funds to help finance the New Deal.

Most of these laws required people in the federal government to put them into action. They formed administrations, which were known as Alphabet Agencies because they were referred to by their initials. For instance, FERA was set up to ensure that the federal relief funds sent out to states were used to add to state relief spending, rather than replace it. Other examples of key Alphabet Agencies are described in the next section.

SOLVING THE AGRICULTURAL CRISIS

ENDING OVER-PRODUCTION

The AAA aimed to raise the price of agricultural goods. It offered **subsidies** to farmers who limited their production. If a farmer kept an acre (4,047 square metres) of land empty, he received around $11 to make up the lost income. As a result, less wheat and cotton were harvested, while demand remained much the same, causing the price to rise.

However, in the short term, this measure did not go far enough. There were still too many farm products from previous harvests stored in warehouses and ready for sale. So, after the First Hundred Days, Roosevelt set up the Commodity Credit Corporation, which paid farmers to keep extra goods in their warehouse. Again, this reduced the amount of farm goods for sale, helping to increase prices. If the price rose above the amount the Corporation had paid, the farmer could buy it back at the original price and sell it at the new, higher price.

KEEPING FARMS
Farmers who struggled to sell their goods also struggled to pay their mortgages. If they stopped mortgage repayments, they lost their farms. In response to this, Roosevelt set up the Farm Credit Administration (FCA). The FCA helped to improve mortgage arrangements for around 20 per cent of the USA's farms, helping farmers to stay on their land.

HELPING INDUSTRY TO RECOVER

Roosevelt's NRA worked with major industries to create industry-wide codes. These set quotas on how much was produced, controlled prices, set wages, limited working hours and banned child labour. Companies were not forced to join the scheme, but many business leaders recognised that the codes would end over-production, stop competitive industries from bankrupting each other and improve working conditions.

However, if businesses ignored the codes, they would be useless, so incentives were offered. Any business that followed a code was allowed to display the symbol of the NRA, the Blue Eagle. The symbol's popularity amongst the public helped ensure 2.3 million businesses took part in the scheme by the end of July 1933. They were proud to show the Blue Eagle at the top of their letters.

Another effect of the National Industrial Recovery Act was that it gave workers the legal right to join unions. This power meant they could join together to fight for better pay, working hours and conditions. In the short term, it caused union membership to rise from 3.1 million in 1932 to 3.9 million in 1939. However, it was not until the Wagner Act (see page 83) that Americans began to form unions in large numbers.

PROVIDING RELIEF TO THE UNEMPLOYED

DIRECT RELIEF
During the First Hundred Days, Congress passed the Federal Emergency Relief Act, providing $500 million for states to spend on relief. Hoover had already offered loans to states, but the new money was a grant, so did not need repaying. It was designed to add to state relief funds and help with the immediate problems created by unemployment. The most pressing need was that unemployed people could not afford to feed their families. Relief helped provide them with a basic income to survive in the short term.

The other serious problem for the unemployed was the risk of being thrown out of their homes. The Home Owner's Refinancing Act was introduced to extend mortgage payments. Instead of the traditional 5 years, homeowners were given 20 years to pay off their mortgage. This extension reduced their monthly payments and made it easier for around 1 million people to keep their homes.

WORK RELIEF

Roosevelt, like the previous president, believed that Americans should be given work rather than handouts. One of his earliest measures was to set up the Civilian Conservation Corps (CCC). This programme took unemployed young men into the countryside and gave them tough outdoor jobs, including trail building and reservoir digging, for $30 a month. Most of this income had to be sent back home, which ensured families benefited from the scheme too.

The CCC was a popular and successful project, demonstrating that Roosevelt planned to put his words into action. Even so, it applied only to 17–23-year-olds, so had employed only 500,000 men by 1935. To help employ greater numbers, Congress established the Public Works Administration (PWA), which was given $3.3 billion of federal money to spend on big construction projects, such as the Grand River Dam in Oklahoma, to create jobs for construction workers.

However, big projects took a long time to get started and the unemployed of 1933 could not wait for them. The head of FERA, Harry Hopkins, recognised that if little had begun by winter, some poor Americans might freeze to death. His solution was a temporary agency, the Civil Works Administration (CWA). With a budget of $400 million, it provided work on short-term projects, like refurbishing schools and road building. By the time it closed in early 1934, it had helped 4.2 million workers survive the winter.

FEDERAL CONTROL

Before 1933, states had been helped by the federal government to solve their own problems and administer their own relief. However, in the South, state governments had not done enough to help the poor. As a result, Roosevelt set up the Tennessee Valley Authority (TVA). It was a huge federal planning agency that would help seven states to recover from the Depression. The TVA aimed to:
- provide work for southerners
- generate and extend coverage of electricity to remote farms
- control flooding and improve the **productivity** of land.

SOURCE E

A photo of the Norris Dam. This dam was the first major project of the TVA and was completed in 1936. It was part of a flood control project, but also generated a large amount of electricity.

The main plan was to build up to 20 dams, supervised by the TVA, which would meet all three aims and redevelop the Tennessee Valley. At the same time, farmers were to be educated in new farming methods and ways to look after the land, while model farms were set up to put these new ideas into action. As a consequence, the problems of drought and dust storms were partly solved, making a similar environmental disaster less likely in the future.

20 March 1933 Economy Act cuts government spending

31 March 1933 Reforestation Relief Act sets up the Civilian Conservation Corps

12 May 1933 Federal Emergency Relief Act starts relief spending programme and sets up Civil Works Authority

13 June 1933 Home Owner's Refinancing Act helps homeowners to extend their mortgage terms

16 June 1933 Farm Credit Act helps farmers to refinance their mortgages

9 March 1933 Emergency Bank Act reorganises US banks

22 March 1933 Beer and Wine Revenue Act legalises the sale of alcohol

12 May 1933 Agricultural Adjustment Act targets agricultural over-production

18 May 1933 Tennessee Valley Authority Act begins a federal programme to redevelop the Tennessee Valley

16 June 1933 National Industrial Recovery Act targets problems in industry and sets up the Public Works Administration

▲ Timeline of major acts passed by Congress during the First Hundred Days

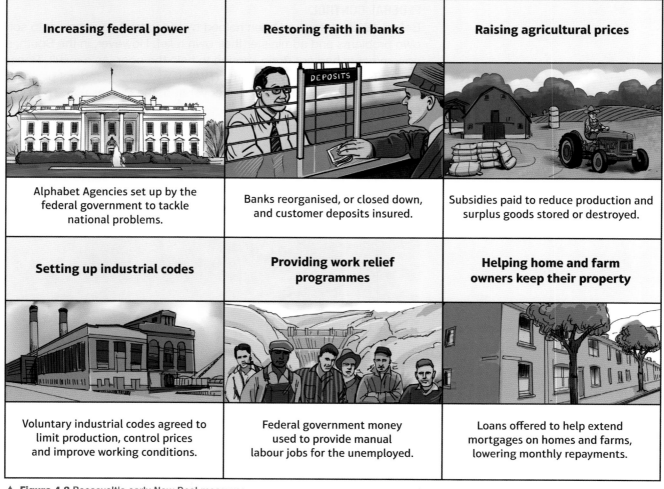

▲ **Figure 4.2** Roosevelt's early New Deal measures

1 Write the script for a fireside chat to promote one of the policies listed on pages 75–78.
2 Read out your script to a partner. After listening, they should be able to identify who your policy will help and how.

EXAM-STYLE QUESTION

Describe **two** key features of the Alphabet Agencies.   **(6 marks)**

A01

HINT

This question targets your ability to demonstrate knowledge and understanding of the key features of the period you have studied.

4.3 THE SECOND NEW DEAL

LEARNING OBJECTIVES

☐ Understand the reasons for the second New Deal

☐ Understand the programmes set up to help the unemployed, the urban poor and farmers

☐ Understand the terms and impact of the Social Security Act, National Labor Relations (Wagner) Act and the Banking Act of 1935.

THE NEED FOR MORE HELP

After 2 years of New Deal programmes, national income was still low, unemployment remained high and workers continued to strike over poor conditions. However, 1935 provided the circumstances for New Dealers to change that. The elections to Congress in November 1934 had brought in politicians who wanted **reform**. At the same time the Supreme Court had shut down some of the agencies of the first New Deal, declaring them unconstitutional (see Chapter 5, page 92). As a result, Roosevelt set out to create a second New Deal, which would:
- provide more work relief for the unemployed
- support workers in industry and improve their rights
- help the rural poor get their own land
- provide for the old during their retirement.

THE WORKS PROGRESS ADMINISTRATION

In May 1935, Roosevelt set up the Works Progress Administration (WPA). He put the man who had planned and organised the CWA, Harry Hopkins, in charge. Roosevelt hoped Hopkins would bring the same burst of activity associated with the CWA to the new agency. Figure 4.3 demonstrates how Hopkins did so through a huge range of short-term work relief projects.

WPA projects helped to employ around 8 million Americans and demonstrated how much the federal government was prepared to spend on relief. During its lifetime, the WPA spent $11 billion, helping poor men and women from both the town and the country, whether they were white or black.

SOURCE F

From a radio broadcast by an assistant commissioner of the WPA, October 1939.

The National Health Survey, one of our greatest WPA projects sponsored by the United States Public Health Service, revealed that every year some 2 million cases of serious illness go entirely without medical treatment. That is why the WPA maintains and assists clinics in most of our cities. That is why it sends nurses into the homes of the poor. That is why it builds hospitals and provides medical and dental treatment for people who could not receive such treatment otherwise.

▶ **Figure 4.3** Projects organised by the WPA

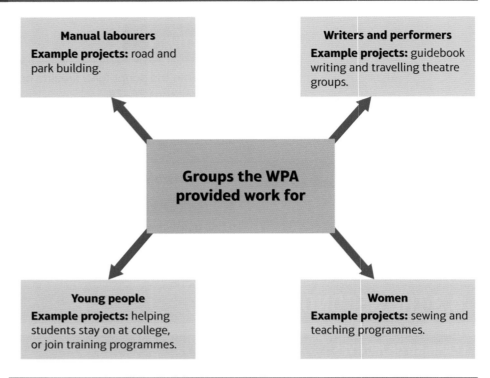

Manual labourers
Example projects: road and park building.

Writers and performers
Example projects: guidebook writing and travelling theatre groups.

Groups the WPA provided work for

Young people
Example projects: helping students stay on at college, or join training programmes.

Women
Example projects: sewing and teaching programmes.

SOURCE G

From an article in a US newspaper published in 1935, with the title *This Business of Relief*.

When the WPA was launched as the solution of the unemployment problem, the President announced that "the federal government must and will quit this business of relief." The new program was to give a job to every able-bodied man whom the new prosperity did not place in private industry. WPA in New York City has put 223,000 persons to work. This still leaves 750,000 unemployed who can hope for no help from WPA, since it has already reached its quota.

EXAM-STYLE QUESTION

AO3

SKILLS ANALYSIS, ADAPTIVE LEARNING, CREATIVITY

Study Sources F and G.
How far does Source F support the evidence of Source G about the success of the Works Project Administration? Explain your answer.   **(8 marks)**

HINT

This question targets your ability to comprehend, interpret and cross-refer sources.

HELP FOR THE POOR

WORK RELIEF

The second New Deal helped the poor to find employment. Work relief projects, including the CCC and PWA, received $4 billion. Along with the newly formed WPA, all of these agencies provided temporary employment for the poor.

EXTEND YOUR KNOWLEDGE

HELPING POOR MUSICIANS

In the 1920s, musicians had played in orchestras to accompany silent films, but the introduction of soundtracks changed all that. Around 70 per cent of musicians lost their jobs and turned to the New Deal for help. The WPA set up the Federal Music Project, which employed 15,000 musicians. It opened up opportunities to perform, such as in the new all-blind orchestra in Mississippi, or to do academic work, including a research project to record black folk music in the South.

HOUSING

Roosevelt also wanted to improve housing conditions. The Resettlement Administration, although set up mainly to help the rural poor, built new suburban towns for urban families. However, only three were constructed, so Congress passed the Housing Act, which set up a new agency to create new homes to replace shanty towns.

WORKING CONDITIONS

A huge part of the second New Deal was the National Labor Relations Act, which was designed to help improve the working lives of industrial workers (see page 83). A few years later, a minimum wage and maximum hours for workers in industry were introduced.

HELP FOR FARMERS

ACCESS TO LAND

Roosevelt wanted the rural poor to have their own farms, rather than working as **sharecroppers** or **tenants** for wealthy landowning farmers. His first measure was the Resettlement Administration, which set out to help resettle families from overworked land. However, this only resettled a few thousand, which led to its replacement by the Farm Security Administration (FSA). The FSA helped the rural poor to buy their own farms and get new equipment to use on them. By 1941, it had offered $1 billion in loans to help farmers.

MIGRANT WORKERS

Until 1935, little had been done to help agricultural workers who did not have their own land or had lost land during the Depression. The FSA now

SOURCE H

A photo of a library in an FSA camp for migrant farm workers from 1938. It shows the WPA librarian in charge.

took action to help migrant workers who travelled across the USA in search of work. They set up migrant camps to provide shelter to those who had left the Dustbowl for California and paid for doctors and dentists to look after migrants. Although this did not help migrants find work, it did help to keep them alive and healthy.

FARM PRICES

The first Agricultural Adjustment Act had been declared not valid by the Supreme Court in 1936, but the price of agricultural goods was still too low. The second Agricultural Adjustment Act created compulsory measures to limit production, using quotas. These were effective because they did not rely on co-operation from farmers. Instead, they were enforced through heavy taxes on sales above the quota, helping the government control how much was produced.

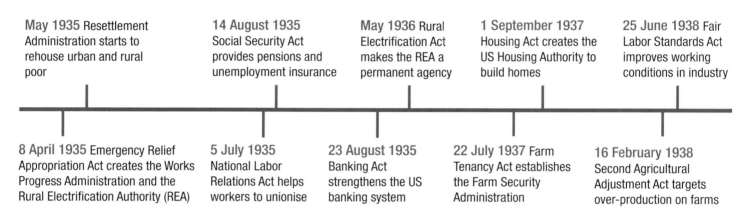

May 1935 Resettlement Administration starts to rehouse urban and rural poor

14 August 1935 Social Security Act provides pensions and unemployment insurance

May 1936 Rural Electrification Act makes the REA a permanent agency

1 September 1937 Housing Act creates the US Housing Authority to build homes

25 June 1938 Fair Labor Standards Act improves working conditions in industry

8 April 1935 Emergency Relief Appropriation Act creates the Works Progress Administration and the Rural Electrification Authority (REA)

5 July 1935 National Labor Relations Act helps workers to unionise

23 August 1935 Banking Act strengthens the US banking system

22 July 1937 Farm Tenancy Act establishes the Farm Security Administration

16 February 1938 Second Agricultural Adjustment Act targets over-production on farms

▲ Timeline of events in the second New Deal

ACTIVITY

1 Look at the first three aims of the second New Deal on page 79. Find an example of a law or agency that was designed to meet each aim.
2 Study Source H and answer the following questions.
  a Which second New Deal programme does the source show?
  b Who were these programmes designed to help?
  c Why would this photo make a good advert for the second New Deal?
3 Use Source H, along with the information in this section, to create a poster promoting the second New Deal.

HELP FOR THE OLD AND DISADVANTAGED

Before 1935, the USA had no national system for pensions or unemployment insurance for workers. It was left to each state to establish a policy that worked for them. In most cases, this meant they had done little. Roosevelt was determined to change this and helped to make the Social Security Act law in 1935. The Social Security Act created:

■ A federal pension system: employees paid into a pension scheme for their retirement, with their contributions matched by a tax on their employer. The contributions were initially 1 per cent of their income, rising to 3 per cent later on.

KEY TERM

matching grant a grant from the federal government that matched the amount the state government paid out

- Federal unemployment insurance: employers of more than eight people paid a tax to the federal government. The money was used to provide unemployment pay for up to 16 weeks at half the normal rate.
- Federal support for disadvantaged groups: support funded by federal **matching grants** provided money for very poor old people, families with dependent children and disabled groups, including blind people.

▼ The impact of the Social Security Act

▼ POSITIVE EFFECTS	▼ NEGATIVE EFFECTS
It was the first nationwide programme to provide pensions and unemployment insurance.	It was self-funded, which meant it could not pay out pensions immediately and the US economy took longer to recover.
$50 million was set aside for the immediate needs of the elderly and $25 million for dependent children.	Pay-outs to disadvantaged groups varied from state to state, because it was funded by matching grants.
By 1939, grants had helped 7,000 children.	Domestic servants and agricultural labourers were not included in the unemployment and pension schemes.

HELP FOR WORKERS

KEY TERMS

closed shop where all employees of a particular company had to join the union chosen by the majority

company unions a union funded by the employer, often created to prevent independent unions from defending the interests of workers

The National Industrial Recovery Act of 1933 had offered some protection to labour unions, but the Supreme Court declared the law invalid in 1935. In its place, Senator Robert Wagner proposed the National Labor Relations Bill. Once it became law, the act, often known as the Wagner Act:

- Strengthened labour unions: workers were legally entitled to join a union and unions could operate **closed shops**. Unfair practices like **company unions** and firing union members were banned.
- Offered federal protection to unions: a National Labor Relations Board (NLRB) was set up, which supervised union negotiations, defended workers who had been fired and helped unions gain recognition from employers.

▼ Impact of the National Labor Relations Act

▼ POSITIVE EFFECTS	▼ NEGATIVE EFFECTS
Union membership rose to around 9 million by 1940.	Many unions had to strike to force companies to recognise them officially.
Before the act, it was mostly skilled craftspeople that joined unions. Now factory workers joined too.	Strikes could be violent, as employers tried to stop them.
The NLRB grew to defend workers. It had 14 lawyers in 1935 and 226 in 1939.	

EXTEND YOUR KNOWLEDGE

MEMORIAL DAY MASSACRE 1937
The steelworkers at a Chicago plant wanted recognition from their employer, Little Steel, but its manager, Thomas Girdler, would not back down. He hired and armed a private police force to control the workers. This action resulted in a bloody incident on Memorial Day, 1937 (the day commemorating those who have lost their lives while serving in America's armed forces). Union supporters had organised a picnic and a peaceful march in front of the plant. However, when they marched, one marcher threw a stick at the police force, triggering a police attack. The force killed ten marchers and injured 30 more, disabling nine of them for life.

SOURCE I

A photo of a strike outside a Chicago steel plant on Memorial Day, 1937. It shows police confronting strikers and sympathisers.

REFORMING BANKS

Roosevelt had managed to rescue the banks in 1933, but as yet there had been no major reforms in their organisation. Control was still divided between the Federal Reserve, the states and the big banks. The Banking Act of 1935 changed that because it:

- created a Board of Governors of the Federal Reserve System chosen by the president
- gave various financial powers to the Board, taking them away from the more powerful banks.

IMPACT OF THE BANKING ACT

KEY TERM

deposit insurance money paid out by the federal government to savers if a bank fails

Despite opposition from bankers who did not want to lose control, the Banking Act strengthened the central banking system. As a result, in 1936 no national bank closed and very little had to be paid out in **deposit insurance**. The US banking system had been modernised and a repeat of the 1929 crisis was far less likely.

EXAM-STYLE QUESTION

A01

Describe **two** key features of the Social Security Act (1935). **(6 marks)**

HINT

This question targets your ability to demonstrate knowledge and understanding of the key features of the period you have studied.

ACTIVITY

1 Create three flow charts, which each begin with a box for the 'problem' (listed below), followed by one for the 'solution' and 'main outcome':
- no national system for pensions or unemployment insurance
- limited access to unions for factory workers
- weak central banking system.
2 Use the material on pages 79–84 to fill in the flow charts.
3 Explain how successful you think each solution was in solving the problems the USA had in 1935.

4.4 RURAL ELECTRIFICATION

LEARNING OBJECTIVES

- Understand the measures set up under the first New Deal to help rural communities receive electricity
- Understand the role of the Rural Electrification Administration in expanding access to electricity across the USA
- Understand the impact of the rural electrification programmes by 1941.

SITUATION BEFORE THE NEW DEAL

Most farms in the USA lacked electricity. In 1930, it was available to around 10 per cent of farms and, in some of the poorest areas, only 1 per cent of farms had it. The problem was that the USA's enormous size meant there were large numbers of remote farms. It was not profitable for private electricity suppliers to run electricity lines to these poor farmers, so they did not bother. This meant farming families had no access to the consumer appliances that were transforming the USA, like electric cookers and fridges. It was also difficult to modernise methods of production, such as keeping chicks in electric **brooders**, because the farmers did not have electricity to power new technologies.

KEY TERM

brooders heated shelters in which chicks are raised

THE NEW DEAL

The first New Deal measure to tackle the problem of rural electrification was the TVA, which built dams to generate electricity and lent money to **co-operatives** to lay power cables. In addition to this, Roosevelt set up the Electric Home and Farm Authority (EHFA), which aimed to help farmers buy electrical appliances. The EHFA encouraged appliance companies to make cheaper models for the TVA area and provided loans, backed by the RFC, to help farmers buy them on an instalment plan.

KEY TERM

co-operative a company that is owned and run by its members to provide something they need

The TVA electrification programme was very popular, which led to its expansion in the second New Deal. From 1935, the Rural Electrification Administration (REA) took over the electrification programme and also made loans to rural co-operatives across the USA.

SOURCE J

From an article by a member of a Rural Electrical Co-operative, written in March 1939, for the *Rural Electrification News*.

I have an old-fashioned body Brussels carpet on my living-room floor, and when I swept it I raised as much dust as if I had been sweeping the dusty pike. When I finished I was choking with the dust, the carpet was not clean, and I was in a bad humor. Now with the vacuum cleaner, I can even dust the furniture before I clean the carpet, the carpet gets clean, and I stay in a good humor.

SOURCE K

A poster to promote the work of the REA from the 1930s. It was a part of a series that advertised the benefits of electricity.

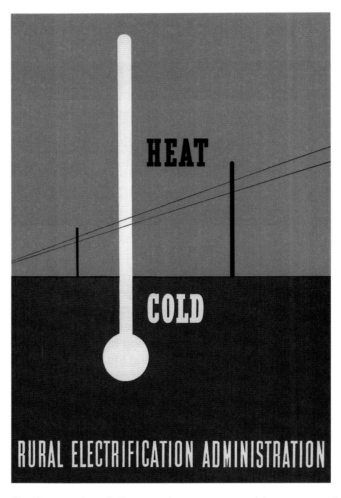

On the one hand, these schemes were a big success, because they:
- Electrified farms: by 1941, 35 per cent of farms had electricity.
- Supported local groups: 417 co-operatives had been helped with loans to lay electric wires for new customers by 1939.
- Boosted demand for electricity: the EHFA, by 1938, had arranged 100,000 contracts for electrical goods.

On the other hand, the progress of rural electrification was slowed down by utility companies, worried about losing profit. These companies tried to stop co-operatives by building **spite lines**, which usually linked up richer communities along a proposed REA route, leaving poorer farms without access. Nevertheless, the REA continued its work and by 1945, 40 per cent of farms had electricity.

KEY TERM

spite line a line carrying electricity built near to proposed co-operatives' lines, which meant any co-operative would struggle to get permission for their line from the REA

SOURCE L

From an article about the TVA in a US magazine, published in 1940. Here the author is writing about a power company's attempt to stop an REA co-operative.

Power company lines were suddenly extended into territory never before serviced and where there were no contracted customers, in an attempt to get prior claims. Service poles were sunk in front yards while residents stood protesting. Lines, dead at both ends, were strung across the plotted way of the cooperative, forcing them to run irregular lengths of wire. Finally, farm wives had to give the cooperative's work gangs shelter by night in their houses, while shotgun brigades guarded the equipment.

EXTRACT A

From a book about Franklin D. Roosevelt, written in 1999.

Also in May 1935 Roosevelt established the Rural Electrification Administration. At this point, some 90 per cent of American farms had no electricity, a luxury enjoyed by city folk. Over the next few years, in part through the formation of co-operatives, this potent form of energy was carried into the countryside, consigning to the past many of the wearisome and centuries-old routines of rural life. Probably no other single measure of the New Deal was as responsible for transforming life in the American South.

EXAM-STYLE QUESTION

A03   **A04**

SKILLS CRITICAL THINKING, REASONING, DECISION MAKING, ADAPTIVE LEARNING, CREATIVITY, INNOVATION

Study Extract A.

Extract A suggests that electrification was a great success.

How far do you agree with this interpretation?

Use Extract A, Sources J and L and your own knowledge to explain your answer. **(16 marks)**

HINT

This question targets your ability to use source material and your own knowledge to evaluate a historical interpretation. Consider the limitations to the success of the REA when exploring the argument against the interpretation.

ACTIVITY

1 Use Sources J and K, as well as the material from Chapter 1 on consumer electronics, to bullet point the ways in which electricity could improve life for a rural family.

2 Arrange yourself into groups of four. Three people should prepare to promote one of the electrification schemes (TVA, EHFA and REA) to the fourth, playing Roosevelt. Consider the following:
   ■ Promoters: explain what your project would involve and why it would have the most significant impact.
   ■ Roosevelt: decide on three criteria to judge the pitches, such as how many people the scheme would help.

3 Perform your pitches in your group. The person playing Roosevelt should decide which one would have the most significant impact and share the reasoning with the group.

RECAP

RECALL QUIZ

1 What were Roosevelt's three aims for the New Deal?
2 How much had Americans deposited in banks after the first month of the New Deal: $500,000, $1 million or $1.5 million?
3 Which Alphabet Agency was set up in 1933 to help raise agricultural prices?
4 What symbol were businesses that followed NRA codes allowed to display?
5 Name a work relief programme created by Roosevelt.
6 List two ways the FSA helped the rural poor.
7 In what year did the Social Security Act, National Labor Relations Act and the Banking Act all become law?
8 Identify one positive impact of the National Labor Relations Act.
9 Who chose the governors of the Federal Reserve after the Banking Act?
10 What percentage of farms had electricity by 1941: 10 per cent, 35 per cent or 40 per cent?

CHECKPOINT

STRENGTHEN

S1 Give an example of a measure taken in 1933 to solve the banking crisis, deal with agriculture, help industry and decrease unemployment.
S2 In what ways was the second New Deal different from the first?
S3 What facts or ideas show that the rural electrification programme was a success?

CHALLENGE

C1 Create a similarities and differences table for the following features:
  ■ the first and second New Deal
  ■ the policies of Hoover (see pages 64–67) and Roosevelt
  ■ life for farmers and factory workers in the 1920s (refer to pages 20–23) and 1930s.
C2 What conclusions can you draw from your table?
C3 Select the one measure from the list which you think was the most effective. Explain why you made this choice.

How confident do you feel about your answers to these questions? If you're not sure you answered them well, try listing the details of each feature to help you identify the similarities and differences.

SUMMARY

■ Roosevelt won the election in 1932 and became president in March 1933.
■ He introduced the New Deal, which aimed to help the economy recover, relieve poverty and reform the way the country was run.
■ Laws were passed during the First Hundred Days to solve the banking crisis and set up the New Deal.
■ Alphabet Agencies, such as the TVA, were established to administer New Deal policies.
■ Agricultural policies tried to reduce the amount of goods produced to help raise prices.
■ The NRA set up codes to help industry recover.
■ More direct relief was given to the poor and work relief projects were set up.
■ The second New Deal expanded work relief programmes and provided help for the rural poor.
■ Reforms were introduced in social security, factory working conditions and the financial system.
■ The REA helped provide electricity to rural households.

EXAM GUIDANCE: PART (B) QUESTIONS

Study Sources A and B

SOURCE A

From a radio broadcast by an assistant commissioner of the WPA, October 1939.

The National Health Survey, one of our greatest WPA projects sponsored by the United States Public Health Service, revealed that every year some 2 million cases of serious illness go entirely without medical treatment. That is why the WPA maintains and assists clinics in most of our cities. That is why it sends nurses into the homes of the poor. That is why it builds hospitals and provides medical and dental treatment for people who could not receive such treatment otherwise.

SOURCE B

From an article in a US newspaper published in 1935, with the title *This Business of Relief*.

When the WPA was launched as the solution of the unemployment problem, the President announced that "the federal government must and will quit this business of relief." The new program was to give a job to every able-bodied man whom the new prosperity did not place in private industry. WPA in New York City has put 223,000 persons to work. This still leaves 750,000 unemployed who can hope for no help from WPA, since it has already reached its quota.

AO3

SKILLS ANALYSIS, ADAPTIVE LEARNING, CREATIVITY

Question to be answered: How far does Source A support the evidence of Source B about the success of the Works Project Administration? Explain your answer. (8 marks)

1 ▶ **Analysis Question 1: What is the question type testing?**
In this question, you have to demonstrate that you can comprehend, interpret and cross-refer sources. In this question, that means you can see similarity and difference between two sources in what they say about the success of the Works Project Administration.

2 ▶ **Analysis Question 2: What do I have to do to answer the question well?**
You have to write about points and areas of agreement and difference between the two sources that you are given. Do NOT be tempted to tell the examiner what each source says. The examiner will already know that! Go straight for the agreements and differences. You might, for example, say, 'The main areas of agreement between the two sources are …', or 'The sources both agree that …' or 'The two sources differ about …'.

3 ▶ **Analysis Question 3: Are there any techniques I can use to make it very clear that I am doing what is needed to be successful?**
This is an 8-mark question, and you need to be sure you leave enough time to answer the (c) part, which is worth 16 marks. So you need to get straight in to your answer. Divide it into three parts. In the first paragraph, identify areas and points of agreement; in the second paragraph, do the same but identify differences. Remember to quote from the source material to support what you are saying. Your final paragraph should explain the extent of the support or agreement between the two sources. That means, how strongly they agree or disagree.

You must identify both agreement and difference. You will get up to 5 marks for doing this and for supporting what you have selected with material from the sources (but a maximum of 4 if you do 'just one side'). There are 3 additional marks for explaining the extent to which one source supports the other.

Answer

The sources both agree on their main subject area, which is that the Works Project Administration did have some success. Source B says that it tried to end direct relief and helped to provide work relief projects for '223,000 people' in New York City. Source A supports this, as it says the WPA was successful in other ways, providing 'medical and dental treatment' for poor people.

The two sources differ in one important way. Source B makes it clear that the WPA was only a partial success when it says 'this still leaves 750,000 unemployed who can hope for no help' in New York City. But Source A only talks about successes, like 'sending nurses into the homes of the poor'. Source A does hint that there are more problems, referring it to '2 million cases of serious illness' that go untreated, but presents this as a successful finding by a WPA research project.

In conclusion, Source A supports the evidence of Source B only in as far as they both agree the WPA achieved some success. However, the lack of support is considerable. Source A is a summary of successes by a WPA assistant commissioner, whereas Source B presents the reality of the project's limited impact on local areas. It is interesting, though, that Source A does not claim to have treated all of the '2 million cases of serious illness', so the sources might not be disagreeing as strongly as it seems at first. But I still think it is true to say that Source A gives very little support to what is said in Source B.

What are the strengths of this answer?
- *The agreements and differences between the sources are clearly identified in separate paragraphs.*
- *The points made in each paragraph are supported by appropriate quotations from the sources.*
- *The conclusion looks at the extent of support Source A gives to Source B.*
- *The comment about 'does not claim' is very perceptive.*

What are the weaknesses of this answer?
- *There are no real weaknesses here, and this is the way to answer such questions. The student just needs to be sure that the answer can be given in no more than 10–15 minutes.*

Answer checklist
- ☐ Identifies similarities
- ☐ Identifies differences
- ☐ Provides information from the sources to support the statements
- ☐ Considers the extent of the support/disagreement. Which is stronger?

5. THE OPPOSITION TO THE NEW DEAL

LEARNING OBJECTIVES

- [ ] Understand the significance of the Supreme Court's opposition to the New Deal for the Alphabet Agencies and Roosevelt's power
- [ ] Understand the effectiveness of opposition from politicians, business leaders and radical critics of the New Deal
- [ ] Understand the achievements and shortcomings of the New Deal, including the impact of the Second World War.

Some Americans thought the New Deal had gone too far. To them, Roosevelt was becoming a dictator, using the Alphabet Agencies to control the USA, while spending huge amounts of government money. Other Americans disagreed. In their eyes, he had not gone far enough, failing to take money from the rich and share it out more equally to the poor. Instead, radical critics wanted Roosevelt to use the Great Depression as an excuse to transform society, not just help it recover. These criticisms cast a shadow over the New Deal, but they did not stop Roosevelt.

Rising above his critics, the president did help the USA to recover from the worst features of the Depression. He even made small steps to help improve the lives of ordinary Americans in the long term. However, problems remained at the end of the 1930s. With little demand for US goods, unemployment high and personal income low, it looked as though the Depression would last forever. It was only when the USA was thrown into another global war that huge government spending, far beyond that of the New Deal, ended the Great Depression once and for all.

5.1 THE OPPOSITION OF THE SUPREME COURT, REPUBLICANS, BUSINESS INTERESTS AND THE LIBERTY LEAGUE

LEARNING OBJECTIVES

- Understand the ways in which the Supreme Court opposed the New Deal and Roosevelt's response
- Understand the reasons for Republican opposition to the New Deal and their successes in the late 1930s
- Understand the objections of business interests to the New Deal and the impact of the American Liberty League.

THE SUPREME COURT

SUMMARY OF THE ALPHABET AGENCIES

AAA: Agricultural Adjustment Administration

CCC: Civilian Conservation Corps

CWA: Civil Works Administration

FERA: Federal Emergency Relief Administration

NLRB: National Labor Relations Board

NRA: National Recovery Administration

PWA: Public Works Administration

REA: Rural Electrification Administration

RFC: Reconstruction Finance Corporation

TVA: Tennessee Valley Authority

The Supreme Court was a major problem for Roosevelt because it had the power to stop New Deal laws. It was run by nine judges who, for the most part, did not share Roosevelt's political views. The majority had been selected by Republicans and could serve for life. The judges they had chosen thought that the US Constitution restricted the power of government, allowing people individual freedom. The Supreme Court believed it had a duty to defend the Constitution and protect the rights of the individual states. It had a responsibility to stop the president and federal government from taking too much power into its own hands.

CHALLENGES TO THE NEW DEAL

To express a view on the New Deal, the Supreme Court had to wait for a business or individual to appeal against an agency or law. Once they had done so, the court could conduct a judicial review, deciding whether the action of an agency or law was constitutional. One of the earliest examples involved the Schechter Poultry Corp., which had signed up to the NRA codes (see Chapter 4, page 76) but then broken the rules about wages and the condition of their birds. The Schechter brothers claimed the federal government had no power over trade within a state and the Supreme Court agreed. Their ruling in what became known as the 'Sick Chicken Case' said that Congress had given too much law-making power to the NRA. This ruling meant the NRA was effectively closed down.

The closure of the NRA threatened the legal basis of the other Alphabet Agencies. For example, in 1936, a cotton processor challenged the AAA, claiming it did not have the power to tax his business. Again, the court found in the company's favour, pointing out that agricultural production should be supervised by the state government, rather than by a federal agency. These two decisions were a major blow to Roosevelt's New Deal, which depended upon greater powers for the federal government.

ROOSEVELT'S RESPONSE

Roosevelt was angered by the actions of the Supreme Court, arguing that it had gone against the views of the American people who had voted for him. His response reflected this anger. He created a plan to appoint new judges to the court who favoured the New Deal. In 1937, he asked Congress for the power to appoint a new judge to replace every current one over the age of 70. As the average age of the judges was 71, he hoped to be able to place six new judges in the Supreme Court straight away, a proposal known as court-packing.

The Supreme Court judges were furious and even Congress thought that Roosevelt was starting to act like the **dictators** of Europe, pushing through his policies at any cost. As a consequence, they defeated his plan, but the Supreme Court got the message. From then on, their decisions began to reflect the public mood and the challenges to the New Deal stopped. Later on, as more judges retired or died, Roosevelt was able to appoint his own more sympathetic judges. The New Deal was now safe from legal challenge.

SOURCE A

A 1937 cartoon about Roosevelt's plan to pack the Supreme Court.

To Six of the Nine

REPUBLICANS

The Republican Party opposed Roosevelt for three main reasons:
- He was a member of the Democratic Party: this was the main opponent to the Republican Party.
- He made the federal government too powerful: they opposed the size and power of the Alphabet Agencies and supported the anti-New Deal decisions of the Supreme Court.
- He spent too much money: the federal government was spending billions of dollars on the New Deal. Republicans did not like using borrowed money to do this or Roosevelt's plan to raise taxes under the Revenue Act of 1935.

KEY TERM

recession a period of falling production, consumption and employment, which is less severe than a depression

EXTEND YOUR KNOWLEDGE

HERBERT HOOVER'S SOCIAL SECURITY NUMBER

Hoover stayed in politics after his election defeat and frequently criticised the New Deal. In the 1936 election campaign, he spoke out against Roosevelt, accusing his government of gathering too much power and setting up communist-style programmes. To make his objections very clear, he refused to apply for a social security number, saying he did not want to be 'numberified'. Despite his objections, Hoover was given a number anyway.

The Republican Party used these arguments to try and defeat Roosevelt in the presidential elections of 1936. Their candidate, Alfred Landon, campaigned for power to be returned to the states, aid for farmers and an end to New Deal regulations. These promises did not appeal to most Americans, so they voted Roosevelt in for a second term as president. However, he struggled to keep their support after a **recession** in 1937 and his unpopular plan to pack the Supreme Court.

SOURCE B

From a speech by Hoover to Republicans, October 1936.

In these instances the Supreme Court, true to their oaths to support the Constitution, saved us temporarily [from the NRA and the AAA]. But Congress in obedience to their oaths should never have passed these acts. The President should never have signed them. But far more important than that, if these men were devoted to the American system of liberty they never would have proposed acts based on the coercion and compulsory organization of men.

SUCCESSFUL OPPOSITION

In 1938, the Republican Party regained the strength they needed to oppose the New Deal because the elections to Congress of that year gave them a lot more seats. They also found that many **conservative** Democrats from states in the South disliked Roosevelt and were willing to join them in a **coalition**. With their support, the Republicans had the power to defeat any new measures that Roosevelt tried to make into law, but not enough votes to remove New Deal legislation completely.

The opponents of the New Deal used their new power to:
- Cut spending on relief programmes: the numbers in federal work relief programmes fell quickly after 1938.
- Investigate Alphabet Agencies: the House of Representatives tried to weaken the WPA and NLRB, accusing officials of being communists.
- Block new measures: a housing plan and a request for more public works projects were rejected in 1939.

In effect, the 1938 elections to Congress had brought the New Deal to a stop. The Fair Labor Standards Act, passed the summer before, would be its last piece of legislation.

BUSINESS OPPOSITION AND THE LIBERTY LEAGUE

Businesses had benefited from the New Deal because it had helped calm an economic crisis. However, as soon as the immediate problems of 1933 were over, they turned against it because:
- They did not like being told what to do: NRA codes and New Deal laws made businesses pay a minimum wage and restrict working hours. This went against the traditional laissez-faire beliefs many businessmen had.
- The New Deal supported unions: the NIRA and Wagner Act gave unions the power to challenge business managers.
- Businesses did not like the way government was spending so much: federal taxes were used to fund New Deal programmes, like the WPA and Social

Security, which businesses did not like. They wanted low taxation so people had more money to buy goods. They believed that was the way to create jobs.

SOURCE C

From an article by a businessman in *Scribner's Magazine*, October 1934.

NRA: Most business men accept the theory of government regulation of private industry, but they resent many of the clumsy methods of *application*. Fine schemes thought out at the top don't work well at the bottom. Toward the agricultural end, the AAA, the feelings are similar. There's fear that the magnitude of the problem is too great for solution by a few minds in Washington.

EXAM-STYLE QUESTION

A03

SKILLS   ANALYSIS, ADAPTIVE LEARNING, CREATIVITY

Study Sources B and C.
How far does Source B support the evidence of Source C about the reasons for opposition to the NRA and AAA? Explain your answer.   **(8 marks)**

HINT

This question targets your ability to comprehend, interpret and cross-refer sources. Think about the attitude to the federal government as a point of agreement between the sources.

SOURCE D

A 1935 cartoon criticising the cost of the New Deal.

OPPOSITION GROUPS

The American Liberty League was founded in 1934. Conservatives from both parties, including the Democrat Al Smith and Republican James Wadsworth, joined with business leaders like the du Pont brothers to oppose the New Deal. They created a national organisation that distributed leaflets, broadcast speeches and sponsored dinners to spread their message. In their view, the New Deal was anti-business and threatened the power of the states. They argued that charities should handle relief and business people who had money should be allowed to keep it.

KEY TERM

Chamber of Commerce a lobbying group dedicated to furthering the interests of businesses in the USA

Their actions were supported by other business groups, who tried to:
- Campaign against Roosevelt: in 1935, the US **Chamber of Commerce** publicly criticised second New Deal legislation like the Wagner Act.
- Sponsor legal challenges to the Alphabet Agencies: the Iron and Steel Institute paid for the Schechter brothers' appeal against the NRA.

Both of these challenges to the New Deal demonstrate how businesses were prepared to use money to weaken it.

LIMITED SUCCESS

Although the American Liberty League spent over $1 million on its organisation and American businesses challenged most pieces of New Deal legislation in the federal courts, their success was limited. The League made little difference for several reasons.
- It struggled to recruit: around 150,000 people joined the League, which was a tiny part of the total population.
- It was unpopular: the Republicans told them to stay out of the 1936 elections because they thought League support would damage their campaign.
- The Supreme Court changed its attitude: after 1937, the court began to support New Deal laws, making the sponsorship of legal challenges a less effective measure.

When, in 1940, the American Liberty League announced the closure of its offices, few Americans noticed its disappearance.

ACTIVITY

1 Study Sources A–D in this section. Write a short description of how each one criticises the New Deal.
2 Create a table with three headings: 'Opposition group', 'Successful' and 'Unsuccessful'. Fill in each column, noting each group's strengths and weaknesses in opposing the New Deal.
3 Explain which opposition group you think was the most effective.

5.2 RADICAL CRITICISM

LEARNING OBJECTIVES

- Understand the criticisms made by radical opponents of the New Deal
- Understand the proposals of Huey Long, Charles Coughlin and other radical critics of the New Deal
- Understand the impact radical criticism had on the second New Deal.

NOTABLE CRITICS OF THE NEW DEAL

Some opponents of the New Deal argued that it did not do enough to tackle the problems of the Great Depression. These included:

- a US senator, Huey Long
- a famous radio priest, Father Charles Coughlin
- a retired health officer, Francis Townsend
- a popular novelist, Upton Sinclair.

Their influence, although short-lived, worried Roosevelt, but also helped him to plan the second New Deal.

HUEY LONG'S SHARE OUR WEALTH PROGRAMME

Huey Long rose to fame as governor of Louisiana. He was popular because he heavily taxed rich people and big businesses in Louisiana. With this money, he provided social services, several years before the New Deal, and introduced reforms to help Louisianans. For instance, he set up an adult reading and writing programme and gave free textbooks to school children. As a consequence, Long's support grew and he was able to win election to Congress as a senator.

After becoming a senator, Long was in a position to criticise the New Deal. His main objections were that:

- the NRA was controlled by big business
- the AAA left poor tenant farmers homeless
- the Social Security Act did not reduce the gap between rich and poor.

This last objection formed the basis of his proposed alternative to the New Deal. His programme was called Share Our Wealth and was set up in early 1934. It involved a heavy tax on the wealthy, taking all of their annual income over $1.8 million away and giving it to ordinary Americans, who were supposed to get a minimum income of $2,500 a year. In effect, it would force the rich to give to the poor.

The problem with Long's Share Our Wealth programme was simple. There were not enough rich people to fund it. Nevertheless, Long was exceptionally popular, as his speechmaking style made ordinary Americans feel like he understood them. In total, an estimated 8 million Americans joined Share Our Wealth Clubs, which made Long very powerful.

If Long had chosen to run in the 1936 presidential election, his huge level of support could have affected the result. However, he was shot dead in September 1935. Share Our Wealth continued under the leadership of Gerald Smith, who joined with Coughlin in the 1936 election, but they met with little success (see page 99).

EXTEND YOUR KNOWLEDGE

EVERY MAN A KING

To boost his popularity, Long published a book, *Every Man a King*, which shone on the shelves with its bright gold cover. In it he presented himself as a champion of the people, claiming his aim in life was to help improve their lives. He had high hopes for it and priced it at $1 so that everyone could buy it. However, ordinary Americans did not buy it. Long had 100,000 printed, but due to poor sales had to give 80,000 copies away.

EXAM-STYLE QUESTION

A01

Describe **two** key features of Huey Long's Share Our Wealth programme.

(6 marks)

HINT

This question targets your ability to demonstrate knowledge and understanding of the key features of the period you have studied.

SOURCE E

From a letter to a New Deal politician, Jim Farley, February 1935. The writer is describing a meeting where Long's name was referred to by the main speaker.

Jim, I never saw a crowd turn loose like that, not for a long time, they just about lifted the roof and amongst them were several that had referred to Long not more than a year ago as a fool and a "nut". Also in the crowd I recognized a lot of local Democrat politicians some who served in New Deal organisations, such as FERA and they were applauding with the rest.

SOURCE F

A photograph from the early 1930s showing Huey Long looking through his fan mail.

FATHER COUGHLIN'S SOCIAL JUSTICE CAMPAIGN

Father Charles Coughlin was a Roman Catholic priest whose parish was near the industrial city of Detroit. His weekly sermons had a national audience because, in 1930, a large radio network gave him a show called *The Golden Hour of the Little Flower*. The show had around 30 million listeners, which meant politicians felt the need to take his opinions seriously. At first, when Coughlin supported the New Deal, millions voted for Roosevelt. Later, when he turned against it, Roosevelt had to find a way to respond to his popular opponent.

Unlike historians, Coughlin had a simple explanation for the Great Depression. It was caused by Wall Street financiers and international bankers. The New Deal was also influenced by them and was, therefore, ineffective. Even worse, he thought communists were responsible for some of its policies and they were using Roosevelt to achieve their aims. As an alternative to the New Deal, Coughlin set up the National Union for **Social Justice** in November 1934. It called for:
- currency and banking reforms
- **nationalisation** of parts of the US economy
- a fairer taxation policy.

To put these ideas into action, Coughlin decided to form a team with Gerald Smith, from Share Our Wealth, and Francis Townsend, from Old Age Revolving Pensions, Ltd (see below). Together they formed the National Union Party and promoted William Lemke as their candidate for president in 1936. Roosevelt was a tough opponent to beat. Lemke got only 828,000 votes compared to Roosevelt's 27.8 million.

Coughlin's failure was largely a result of the second New Deal. In 1935, Roosevelt put in place some of the reforms that Long and Coughlin had campaigned for, which made it more difficult for radicals to criticise him. Coughlin also struggled to remain popular because his broadcasts attacked a well-liked president and were increasingly **anti-Semitic**. As a consequence, once the National Union Party had lost the election, Coughlin's influence on politics declined too.

KEY TERM

social justice the idea of working towards a fairer society

SOURCE G

From a letter by an Alabama farmer, Elmer Woods, 1935. He is describing his attitude to plans like those of Huey Long and Father Coughlin.

We has read your letter and we has studied over your program. We think the program is too radical. You all believe for equal rights for black people and you alls program sounds communist... If we has looked at it wrongly or if there is some more to understand we would like to know. Otherwise I guess we won't be interested. We think you all mean right but its to radical.

EXTEND YOUR KNOWLEDGE

COUGHLIN'S ANTI-SEMITISM
After 1938, Coughlin's radio broadcasts and articles in his newspaper, *Social Justice*, began to criticise Jewish people. His anti-Semitic views led him to accuse Jewish people of causing the Depression. He praised Hitler, even using parts of a speech by his propaganda minister. Such views were not very popular in the USA where there were many Jewish people. In 1940, his radio broadcasts were banned and, 2 years later, so was his newspaper. After threats of arrest from the government for encouraging rebellion, Coughlin finally gave up and stopped writing.

OTHER RADICAL CRITICS

DR FRANCIS TOWNSEND
In late 1933, Dr Francis Townsend, a retired public health officer, was shocked by the sight of three elderly women searching through bins for bits of leftover food. This, he claimed, made him want to work against poverty amongst the elderly. He came up with the idea for Old Age Revolving Pensions, Ltd. He

proposed that everyone over the age of 60 should get $200 a month to spend within 30 days. It would be funded by a 2 per cent sales tax but the elderly people would spend the money and this would in turn help the economy to grow.

On first inspection, Townsend's idea seemed like a good one. Old people were sensible spenders and would benefit from the income. If you did not study the figures too closely, it even sounded possible, which is why 500,000 people joined Townsend clubs and 20 million Americans signed a **petition** to support the plan. However, on closer inspection, the numbers made no sense. There was no way that such a huge pension could be funded by such a small tax, which is why it could not seriously challenge Roosevelt's proposed Social Security Act.

Tax the rich and give to the poor.

Senator Huey Long

Give the government even more power to fix the economy.

Father Charles Coughlin

Provide over-60s with $200 a month to boost consumer spending.

Doctor Francis Townsend

Let poor people farm empty land and run abandoned factories.

Upton Sinclair

▶ **Figure 5.1** Radical critics of the New Deal

UPTON SINCLAIR

Another radical opponent was the novelist, Upton Sinclair. His most well-known book, *The Jungle*, exposed poor conditions for workers in the meat-packing industry. He used his fame to run for governor in California in 1934, using the slogan 'End Poverty In California' (EPIC). He argued that empty land and shut-down factories should be opened up for the unemployed to use. To ease their poverty, they would produce what they needed. It was an attractive idea, but it was seen as too radical, so Californians elected the Republican candidate instead.

IMPACT OF CRITICISM

Roosevelt's radical opponents challenged his popularity, but they were not serious blocks to the New Deal. Unlike the Supreme Court or the Republicans, they could not vote down his policies. However, they did influence them. The Social Security Act, the National Labor Relations Act and the Revenue Act of 1935 were all responses to Long, Coughlin and Townsend's criticisms of the first New Deal. This is why their movements struggled after 1935. When their suggestions looked similar to Roosevelt's, Americans had fewer reasons to listen to them.

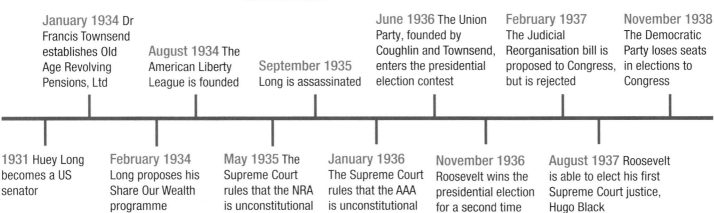

January 1934 Dr Francis Townsend establishes Old Age Revolving Pensions, Ltd

August 1934 The American Liberty League is founded

September 1935 Long is assassinated

June 1936 The Union Party, founded by Coughlin and Townsend, enters the presidential election contest

February 1937 The Judicial Reorganisation bill is proposed to Congress, but is rejected

November 1938 The Democratic Party loses seats in elections to Congress

1931 Huey Long becomes a US senator

February 1934 Long proposes his Share Our Wealth programme

May 1935 The Supreme Court rules that the NRA is unconstitutional

January 1936 The Supreme Court rules that the AAA is unconstitutional

November 1936 Roosevelt wins the presidential election for a second time

August 1937 Roosevelt is able to elect his first Supreme Court justice, Hugo Black

▲ Timeline of opposition to the New Deal

EXTRACT A

From a history of the United States, published in 2013.

The New Deal was popular with many people. President Roosevelt had millions of letters of support during his presidency. However, he also faced opposition from the very beginning. Why? Some opponents of FDR felt he wasn't going far enough. They said he should nationalise banks, make stronger laws against big business and introduce social reforms such as pensions and unemployment benefit. Two of these critics [Long and Coughlin] had a lot of public support and FDR feared their opposition would damage his reputation, especially as they had supported him in 1932.

EXAM-STYLE QUESTION

A03 **A04**

SKILLS | CRITICAL THINKING, REASONING, DECISION MAKING, ADAPTIVE LEARNING, CREATIVITY, INNOVATION

Study Extract A.
Extract A suggests that Long and Coughlin had a lot of public support. How far do you agree with this interpretation?
Use Extract A, Sources E and G and your own knowledge to explain your answer.

(16 marks)

HINT

This question targets your ability to use source material and your own knowledge to evaluate an historical interpretation.

ACTIVITY

1 Create a campaign leaflet for one of the radical critics, which describes:
■ what is wrong with Roosevelt's New Deal
■ what you propose
■ who your proposal will help (the poor, the elderly, the unemployed or most Americans)
■ how it will help them.
2 Create a table with three columns: 'Critic', 'Criticism of the New Deal' and 'Proposal'. Swap leaflets with other members of the class to help fill it in.
3 Make your own copy of Figure 5.1 Add a further sentence of detail to each of the speech bubbles.

5.3 THE ACHIEVEMENTS AND SHORTCOMINGS OF THE NEW DEAL

LEARNING OBJECTIVES

■ Understand the extent to which the New Deal achieved the aims of recovery, relief and reform
■ Understand the achievements and shortcomings of the New Deal for women, black people and Native Americans
■ Understand the impact of the Second World War on the USA's recovery from the Great Depression.

THE END OF THE NEW DEAL

In January 1939, Roosevelt made a speech to Congress. For the first time since 1933, he made no mention of a New Deal policy. Although many of the Alphabet Agencies continued to operate, his programme of economic and social reform was closing down. In its place, the start of the Second World War became the focus of his presidency.

NEW DEAL AIM 1: RECOVERY

ACHIEVEMENTS

The New Deal had set out to raise farm income, increase industrial production and end the banking crisis. During the 1930s, farm income had risen from $2.6 billion a year to $4.6 billion and farmers had received $4 billion of direct help from the government. Industry had also begun to recover as most businesses that survived after 1933 were able to make a profit. Finally, the RFC helped 6,000 banks to reopen after their forced closure in March 1933. As a result, the New Deal helped unemployment fall from 12.8 million in 1933 to 9.5 million by 1939.

A 1934 cartoon showing Roosevelt steering the USA towards recovery, but his critics continuing to oppose him.

tenant farmers farmers who rent their land, paying the landlord in the form of cash or a share of crops

SHORTCOMINGS

Despite these successes, problems remained in all three areas.

■ **Farming**: farm income rarely reached 1929 levels during the 1930s, **tenant farmers** were thrown off their land and the recovery relied on regular government payments.

■ **Industry**: the NRA codes did not work as many businesses ignored them. Old industries, like coal and textiles, remained unprofitable and the entire country experienced a deep recession in 1937–38.

■ **Banking**: despite help from the RFC, 106 banks that had received extra funds were forced to close.

By the end of the 1930s, the economy had still not fully recovered. Even though unemployment had fallen, it was still at 17.2 per cent in 1939 compared to 3.2 per cent in 1929.

▼ US government statistics: unemployment from selected years 1929–41

YEAR	NUMBER UNEMPLOYED	PERCENTAGE OF ALL THOSE WORKING
1929	1,550,000	3.2
1933	12,830,000	24.9
1935	10,610,000	20.1
1937	7,700,000	14.3
1938	10,390,000	19.0
1941	5,560,000	9.9

NEW DEAL AIM 2: RELIEF

In 1933, Americans had been promised direct federal relief and work relief. The following table lists the successes and failures of the New Deal in keeping this promise.

▼ Achievements and shortcomings of the New Deal's relief policies

▼ AIM	▼ ACHIEVEMENTS	▼ SHORTCOMINGS
Provide work relief programmes	The WPA employed 8 million people. The work relief projects created new parks, roads and schools.	The projects relied heavily on government spending. The work relief projects provided work for only about 40 per cent in need of it.
Provide direct relief to the poor	Thirty five per cent of the population received relief from the government. The Social Security Act provided unemployment insurance for the first time.	The government did not spend enough on relief. Relief varied from state to state. The poor needed social housing, but the government built little.

The table demonstrates that the New Deal did provide far more relief than had been offered by Hoover. The problem was that the USA's recovery seemed to rely upon government spending. When in 1937 Roosevelt tried to cut spending, unemployment rose by around 5 per cent. The president had to go back to Congress to ask for $3 billion more to spend on work relief again. Until the Second World War increased demand for factory and agricultural workers, the New Deal had made many Americans dependent on relief.

NEW DEAL AIM 3: REFORM

The New Deal brought much-needed reforms to the USA. These included the following.
- Social security: for the first time, the federal government provided help to families, the elderly, the unemployed and the disabled.
- The treatment of industrial labour: unions were recognised, minimum wages introduced and working hours limited.
- The living conditions of agricultural workers: many families were provided with electricity, had their land improved and were given financial help to keep it.
- Financial regulations: the banking system was centralised and greater controls were placed on the stock market.

However, there were limits to the amount of reform Roosevelt introduced. The social security system left out large groups of people, including agricultural workers and household servants, and the payments were relatively small. The New Deal also did little to reduce the gap between rich and poor. Most social security was paid for out of people's wages, rather than federal money. This system meant taxation was not used to take money from richer people and give it to the poor. As a consequence, by 1940, the gap remained much the same as it was in 1930.

EXTEND YOUR KNOWLEDGE

TAXING THE RICH
Roosevelt tried to make taxation fairer. In 1935, he asked high earners to pay more tax. He also tried to limit the ways in which people could avoid paying tax. However, rich Americans had a lot of power. This meant the plans met with fierce opposition in Congress, which disliked some of the most radical features. They lowered the proposed rates, protected untaxed accounts and blocked an inheritance tax. The rich were clearly not as ready for reform as the poor.

WOMEN, BLACK PEOPLE AND NATIVE AMERICANS

A person's background had a huge effect on how the New Deal changed their lives. Figure 5.2 shows the achievements and shortcomings of Roosevelt's actions for women, black people and Native Americans.

Achievements	Group	Shortcomings
• More influence in politics because of the work of Roosevelt's wife, Eleanor. • Given specific help by the Women's and Professional Division in the WPA. • Grants provided for women with dependent children due to the Social Security Act.	Women	• Paid less than men: in 1937, a woman earned around half a man's wage. • The number of women in professional jobs fell from 14.2% to 12.3%. • Alphabet Agencies provided more help for men: the CCC created 2.5 million jobs for men, whereas camps for women offered only 5,000 places a year.
• A 'Black Cabinet' gave black people more political power. • 30% of black families received relief. • Early signs of the end of segregation, as some CCC camps were integrated.	Black people	• The AAA forced black tenants off farmland and the NRA caused many black people to lose their jobs. • Relief payments were often lower than those given to white people. • Most black workers had no access to social security.
• The Indian Reorganization Act (1934) restored 7.4 million acres of land to tribes. • Native Americans were given a chance to vote and govern themselves. • The new law recognised the right of Native American women to vote.	Native Americans	• Some New Deal policies, such as a plan to kill large numbers of the Navajo tribe's sheep and goats, were unpopular. • Most were still very poor. • Reliance on New Deal agencies, like the WPA, left Native Americans without help when they closed down.

▲ **Figure 5.2** Groups affected by the New Deal

KEY TERM

Black Cabinet a group of around 100 black people, who had been given positions in Roosevelt's government and tried to influence government policies towards black people

SOURCE I

From an article by a member of Roosevelt's **Black Cabinet**, written in 1941, about black people and the CCC.

250,000 black youth have served in the corps since President Roosevelt initiated the Civilian Conservation Corps in 1933.

$700,000 a month for the past year has been allotted by black CCC boys to their parents and dependents back home.

2,000 black project assistants' leaders and assistant leaders are on duty at CCC Camps.

147 black college graduates are serving CCC camps as educational advisers.

SOURCE J

From an article about the CCC in a US magazine published in 1935 with the title *A Negro in the CCC*.

Before we left the bus the officer shouted: "Colored boys fall out in the rear." The colored from several buses were herded together, and stood in line until after the white boys had been registered and taken to their tents. This seemed to be the established order at Camp Dix. This separation of the colored from the whites was rigidly maintained. Our tents were the worst in Camp Dix. Old, patched, without floors or electric lights.

EXAM-STYLE QUESTION

A03

SKILLS ANALYSIS, ADAPTIVE LEARNING, CREATIVITY

Study Sources I and J.
How far does Source I support the evidence of Source J about the treatment of black people in the USA during the New Deal?
Explain your answer.

(8 marks)

HINT

This question targets your ability to comprehend, interpret and cross-refer sources.

THE SECOND WORLD WAR AND THE NEW DEAL

The New Deal was not the only reason the American economy began to recover. Another was the Second World War. The USA did not enter the war until 1941, but even before then, Roosevelt took action to try to prevent the Allies being defeated by Hitler. In 1939, he convinced Congress to allow the USA to sell military supplies to Britain and the Allies. Then, in 1941, Congress passed the Lend-Lease Act. This law allowed the USA to lend war supplies to any country which might prevent a Nazi attack on the USA. As a result, a large number of jobs were created in both industry and agriculture, to meet the needs of the Allies.

IMPACT OF THE SECOND WORLD WAR

Politicians were prepared to enter into far greater debt to protect themselves than they had been to support the New Deal. The jobs created by government spending on defence meant unemployment fell from around 9.5 million in 1939 to 5.5 million in 1941. At the same time, the war helped the USA to recover from:

■ Low farm incomes: the overall income on US farms rose by around 50 per cent between 1939 and 1941.

■ A lack of demand for American products: in the first 3 years of the war, US exports grew by over 70 per cent.
■ Dependency on work relief: the number of people on work relief fell from around 3.3 million in 1939 to 2.2 million in 1941.

These improvements demonstrate that, while the New Deal eased the pain of the Great Depression in the 1930s, the Second World War made long-term recovery possible.

ACTIVITY

1 Create three spider diagrams with a New Deal aim in the centre of each and two branches for achievements and shortcomings. Add notes to each diagram.
2 In pairs, imagine you are playing a game of verbal table tennis. One of you supports the New Deal, the other opposes it.
   ■ Supporter serves first: tell your opponent an achievement of the New Deal.
   ■ The opposition returns the serve: tell your opponent a shortcoming linked to that achievement.
3 Keep playing until one of you runs out of arguments and loses.
4 Draw a diagram that summarises your match.

RECAP

RECALL QUIZ

1 Which Alphabet Agency was closed down after the Schechter Poultry Corp. case in the Supreme Court?
2 How many new judges did Roosevelt want to appoint to the Supreme Court: six, 12 or 100?
3 Name the Republican candidate who stood against Roosevelt in the 1936 presidential election.
4 In what year did the Republicans gain a lot more seats in Congress?
5 Name the organisation that the du Ponts helped to found to oppose the New Deal.
6 How much was the minimum income Huey Long offered American families: $100, $1,000 or $2,500?
7 Which Roman Catholic priest established the National Union for Social Justice?
8 Which group of Americans did Dr Francis Townsend want to help: pensioners, black people or women?
9 What had unemployment fallen to by 1939: 6 million, 9.5 million or 12.8 million?
10 Which event ended the Great Depression in the USA?

CHECKPOINT

STRENGTHEN
S1 What examples can you find of Supreme Court opposition to the New Deal?
S2 Select three different opponents of the New Deal and summarise their actions.
S3 List two ways in which the New Deal was a success and two in which it was a failure.

CHALLENGE
C1 Create nine diamonds. Using this chapter, select nine different groups affected by the New Deal, such as judges and farmers, to put on each diamond.
C2 Rank your diamonds according to how much the New Deal helped each group. If it had a highly beneficial effect, put the diamond at the top. If it created problems for the group, put it at the bottom.
C3 In no more than 150 words, write an explanation of whether the New Deal was a success or a failure. Refer to different groups in your response.

SUMMARY

■ The Supreme Court closed down the NRA and the AAA.
■ Roosevelt's attempt to appoint new judges sympathetic to the New Deal was stopped by Congress in 1937.
■ Republicans opposed the New Deal because it was too expensive and gave the president too much power.
■ The Republican Party gained more seats in the elections of 1938, helping them to block any more New Deal legislation.
■ Business interests joined with politicians to form an anti-New Deal organisation called the American Liberty League (1934).
■ Huey Long's Share Our Wealth programme (1934) proposed a tax on the rich to provide Americans with a minimum income.
■ Father Coughlin's Social Justice Campaign wanted financial reforms and nationalisation.
■ Other radical critics proposed a revolving pension and a programme to help end poverty.
■ The New Deal did ensure some economic recovery, provided large amounts of relief and secured a few long-term reforms.
■ The Second World War led to huge government spending, ending the Great Depression in the USA.

EXAM GUIDANCE: PART (C) QUESTIONS

Study Extract C.

EXTRACT C

From a history of the United States, published in 2013.

Many people still believed in *laissez faire*, saying relief was not 'the American way', it just encouraged people to be lazy. Many businesses deeply resented the NRA codes and the fines imposed for breaking them. Some chose to work outside the NRA, but lost customers as a result. Some Republicans supported the New Deal, but many still supported *laissez faire*. Even more were suspicious of federal control, fearing it was a step towards communism, which had taken over in the USSR and which it was believed had many followers in the USA.

SOURCE A

From a speech by Hoover to Republicans, October 1936.

In these instances the Supreme Court, true to their oaths to support the Constitution, saved us temporarily [from the NRA and the AAA]. But Congress in obedience to their oaths should never have passed these acts. The President should never have signed them. But far more important than that, if these men were devoted to the American system of liberty they never would have proposed acts based on the coercion and compulsory organization of men.

SOURCE B

From an article by a businessman in *Scribner's Magazine*, October 1934.

NRA: Most business men accept the *theory* of government regulation of private industry, but they resent many of the clumsy methods of *application*. Fine schemes thought out at the top don't work well at the bottom. Toward the agricultural end, the AAA, the feelings are similar. There's fear that the magnitude of the problem is too great for solution by a few minds in Washington.

A03 **A04**

SKILLS CRITICAL THINKING, REASONING, DECISION MAKING, ADAPTIVE LEARNING, CREATIVITY, INNOVATION

Question to be answered: Extract C suggests that businesses and Republicans opposed the New Deal because they supported laissez faire.

How far do you agree with this interpretation?

Use Extract C, Sources A and B and your own knowledge to explain your answer. (16 marks)

Analysis Question: What do I have to do to answer this question well?
- You have to demonstrate that you can use two sources and your own knowledge in order to show how far you agree with a historian's interpretation of an event.
- This is a 16-mark question and you must make sure you write a quick plan before you start. This is because it is important to organise your ideas and your own knowledge.
- Do NOT be tempted to write all you know about the topic, but select those parts of your own knowledge that are directly relevant to the interpretation given in the question.

Your answer could take a different approach to that at the end of Chapter 3 and look like this.

Paragraph 1: show how the sources agree with the interpretation, and use your own knowledge to support this evaluation.

Paragraph 2: show how the sources disagree with the interpretation and use your own knowledge to support this evaluation.

Paragraph 3: reach an overall judgement that is supported by brief references to the most important points you have made in paragraphs 1 and 2.

Answer

Most of the sources agree that people who opposed the New Deal supported laissez-faire ideas. Source A shows the Republicans did not like the NRA and AAA. This was because they set too many limits on what businesses and farmers could do. Extract C says that 'many people still believed in laissez-faire', which is true because they voted in more Republicans to Congress in the 1938 elections. This suggests that most people must have supported their ideas.

However, there were other reasons why businessmen and Republicans opposed the New Deal. Both Source A and Extract C say it threatened people's freedom. In Source A it talks about the 'system of liberty', which was damaged by giving too much power to the federal government. Extract C backs this up because it says people 'were suspicious of federal control', which the New Deal strengthened. For example, the TVA controlled planning for seven US states. Source B gives an alternative argument for why there was opposition from businessmen. It says that it was poorly set up. This is true, as NRA codes were ignored by many businesses and the AAA was seen as wasteful, destroying crops and killing animals.

So, while it is true laissez-faire was an important reason for opposition, it was not the only one.

What are the strengths of this answer?
- *A sound understanding is shown of the two sources and the extract.*
- *It follows a clear structure, looking at both agreement and disagreement with the interpretation.*
- *Relevant contextual knowledge is used in support of the points made.*
- *The interpretation is both supported and challenged by the use of contextual knowledge where it goes beyond the information contained in the sources.*

What are the weaknesses of this answer?
- *The answer looks at the arguments for and against the interpretation using the two sources, own knowledge and the extract itself, but it does not give a satisfactory conclusion. It still needs to explain 'how far'.*
- *To get the very highest marks, the answer has to do more than say 'yes and no'. It has to build up a line of reasoning. For example, the first paragraph builds up the view that there was support for laissez-faire, but the second one could argue businessmen and Republicans also believed the government misused its power.*

Answer checklist
- ☐ Identifies agreement and disagreement with the hypothesis
- ☐ Uses information from the two sources, the extract and own contextual knowledge
- ☐ Addresses 'how far?' by 'weighing' the evidence to see which side is most strongly supported.

GLOSSARY

adulterers people who are married and have sex with someone who is not their wife or husband

agnostic someone who believes that people cannot know whether God exists or not

anti-Semitic views that show a hatred of Jewish people

baptise to accept someone as a member of a particular Christian church by a ceremony of baptism

bankrupt without enough money to pay what you owe

broker someone who buys and sells things such as shares in companies or foreign money for other people

chaperone someone who accompanies a person (often an older woman accompanying a younger women)

coalition group of people who join together to achieve a particular purpose, usually a political one

colonies countries or areas under the political control of a more powerful country, usually one that is far away

Congress the group of people chosen or elected to make laws in the USA

conservative not liking changes or new ideas

consumerism the belief that it is good to buy and use a lot of goods and services

deported to make someone leave a country and return to the country they came from, especially because they do not have a legal right to stay

dictators rulers who have complete power over countries, especially where power has been gained by force

discrimination treating people unfairly because of their group or class

diversity the fact of including many different types of people or things

electrocution the act of killing someone using electricity

empire a group of countries that are all controlled by one ruler or government

enforcement when people are made to obey a rule, law, etc.

ethnic relating to a particular race, nation, or tribe and their customs and traditions

evangelist someone who travels to different places and tries to persuade people to become Christians

evolutionary relating to the way in which plants and animals develop and change gradually over a long period of time

flappers fashionable young women in the late 1920s

fundamentalists people who follow religious laws very strictly

ghettos parts of a city where people of a particular race or class, especially people who are poor, live separately from the rest of the people in the city

incentives things that encourage you to work harder, start a new activity, etc.

innovations new ideas, methods or inventions

instalments a series of regular payments that you make until you have paid all the money you owe

insure to buy insurance so that you will receive money if something bad happens to you, your family, your possessions, etc.

kidnap to take someone somewhere illegally by force, often in order to get money for returning them

labour all the people who work for a company or in a country

legislation a law or set of laws

loan sharks people who lend money at very high rates of interest and will often use threats or violence to get the money back

marketing the activity of deciding how to advertise a product, what price to charge for it, etc.

mechanisation the act of changing a system or process to use machines instead of people or animals

melting pot a place where a variety of people and cultures mix together in one society

middle class the social class that includes people who are educated and work in professional jobs, for example teachers or managers

mortgages legal arrangements by which people borrow money from a bank or similar organisation in order to buy a house, and pay back the money over a period of years

nationalisation the act of bringing a company or industry under the control of a government

persecution cruel or unfair treatment of someone over a period of time, especially because of their religious or political beliefs

petition a written request signed by a lot of people, asking someone in authority to do something or change something

productivity the amount produced by a group of workers over a given time

prosecution when a charge is made against someone for a crime, or when someone is judged for a crime in a court of law

quotas official limits on the number or amount of something that is allowed in a particular period

racist prejudice against someone because of their race

radical someone who is radical has ideas that are very new and different, and against what most people think or believe

raids surprise visits made to a place by the police to search for something illegal

reform a change or changes made to a system or organisation in order to improve it

republic a country governed by elected representatives of the people, and led by a president, not a king or queen

restricted limited or controlled, especially by laws or rules

riots situations in which large crowds of people are behaving in a violent and uncontrolled way, especially when protesting against something

segregate to separate one group of people from others, especially because they are of a different race, sex or religion

self-sufficient able to provide all the things you need without help from other people

shanty town a very poor area in or near a town where people live in small houses made from thin sheets of wood, tin, etc.

sharecroppers farmers who use someone else's land and give the owner part of the crop in return

shareholders people who own shares in a company or business

slogan a short phrase that is easy to remember and is used in advertisements, or by politicians, organisations, etc.

subsidies money that is paid by a government or organisation to make prices lower, reduce the cost of producing goods, etc.

suburban related to a suburb, or in a suburb

supremacy the position in which you are more powerful or advanced than anyone else

Supreme Court the most important court of law in some states of the USA

teargassed affected by tear gas that stings your eyes, used by the police or army to control crowds

tenants people who live in a house, room, etc. and pay rent to the person who owns it

testified made a formal statement of what is true, especially in a court of law

tonnes unit for measuring weight, 1 tonne being equal to 1,000 kilograms

unions organisations formed by workers to protect their rights

unrest a political situation in which people protest or behave violently

upper class the group of people who belong to the highest social class

workforce all the people who work in a particular industry or company, or are available to work in a particular country or area

working class the group of people in society who traditionally do physical work and do not have much money or power

workshop a room or building where tools and machines are used for making or repairing things

INDEX